City of Coloured Lights

SILVER O'CITY

 FriesenPress

Suite 300 - 990 Fort St
Victoria, BC, V8V 3K2
Canada

www.friesenpress.com

ISBN
978-1-77097-181-3 (Hardcover)
978-1-77097-182-0 (Paperback)
978-1-77097-183-7 (eBook)

1. POETRY, AFRICAN

Distributed to the trade by The Ingram Book Company

City of
Coloured
Lights

PREFACE

I was shown an empty throne
In the great congregation,
And a robe hung by its arm,
Loose.
I was shown the city of colored lights,
Where flowers and carpets of greener grass
Sing the songs of the beloved.
And my winged guide
Turned to me and
Without a mouth opened
Uttered, "It's all yours ..."

Silver O'City, The City of Coloured Lights (Abner Mwaka Owor)

While at Nairobi University, I presented my early poems to Okot P'Bitek and Taban Lo-lyong, who at that time lectured there. My more literary-oriented friend and peer at the university, Dr. Aloo Mojola, perfected my academic and technical poetry writing. These poems were immediately acclaimed in the East African literary scene, and some were published with other notable Kenyan poets in the book *Singing with the Night* (ed. Chris Wangala), which now serves as a university teaching resource.

In Nairobi, I pioneered contemporary gospel music in the region through my band, The Trekkers, leading the group for six years. In 1979, I was admitted to the University of Edinburgh to study Urban and Regional Planning. While there, I engaged in more poetry writing and presenting.

At the Edinburgh City Fellowship Church, I received special appreciation and encouragement, especially from the elder Dr. Phil. Moore. I had opportunity to read poems on many occasions, and they were highly applauded. This convinced me of the impact of modern poetry and the arts. When I attended a performing arts Christian camp in Green Belt, England, I further discovered how deeply ordinary, non-literary folk could appreciate modern poetry. The poems presented were relevant to the daily events in their lives. From there, I realized the need to expand the themes of my own poems to cover widely diverse themes in human experience, like love and romance, nature, work, faith, and politics. At that time, many of these areas were taboo in Christian circles.

Every area of Uganda has its own way of understanding and expressing things; however, if something isn't articulated or written down, it can't be properly explored. Communicating different perspectives enables a culture to develop its beauty and intellectual power to greater heights. Poetry is a powerful tool in this empowerment. It enables one to concisely say many complicated things in one sentence. For example, the rottenness of thirty years of independent Uganda's political system was aptly described discernibly in the title of Alex Mukulu's play, *Thirty Years of Bananas.* In one of my poems on the beauty and excellence of Uganda, I say:

"Sir Winston Churchill was neither drunk nor asleep when he said Uganda is 'The Pearl of Africa.'" In my poem "Sahara Body," I say in a few words what could otherwise take thousands of desperate letters to say: "Your body is sand dunes to me." The title of the poem "Cosmic Sergeant Major" succinctly identifies the warped understanding most people have of God.

Many of my poems have been recited and applauded in large public gatherings. From there I began to compile many more poems. There were, however, long wilderness years when, through hindsight, I realize that God was revealing to me a new understanding of Kingdom-of-God living. I began to see the contribution poetry and other literary works could make to national transformation.

Silver O'City

INTRODUCTION

This book is a prophetic word of God; it speaks the mind of God, in poetic form, for this generation—a generation believed by many to be the last-days generation. The poems contain a wide range of literary forms, such as metaphors, allegories, songs, codes, pictures, and parables. The prophets of old, the early disciples, and even some modern-time prophets of God, such as the late Kim Clement, Mark Taylor, and others communicate the mind of God using such indirect renderings. These vary from the simplistic and common to the highly complex and academic.

The Bible says that the Lord Jesus taught often using parables, simple stories that common folk could understand but with hidden and deep meanings about the Kingdom. Some of the meanings were so concealed, the Lord later had to later untangle them for His disciples. This was deliberate. People remember such stories better and eventually understand their deeper meaning. Many traditional cultures possess colourfully folktales and songs, crafted for the next generations to remember and glean their profound intentions.

Throughout this book, I utilize a number of poetic styles and various levels of complexity; however, aware that most Christian readers may be unfamiliar with poetry, I also use a fair number of the simpler and entertaining forms. For example, in poems like "Zanzibar," "Myriad Sights (of India)," and "Changing Shape of a Cloud," I apply simple and fresh-faced poetry steeped with meaning. At another level, again with the intention of imprinting certain images or dogma, I apply various graphic and typographic layouts to the poems. Poems like "Murchison Falls National Park," "Who Cares," "Love Trap," and "Sample S's" are written in deliberate visual forms. I also play with words beyond traditional poetic rhythms. In the poem "Melting Sun," I wrote verses such as: bridegroom, born in Bethlehem, bigger brother; best.

At the enigmatic end, I start with the Bible position that it is the prerogative of God to hide things, and our job is to search them out. Likewise, poetry deliberately hides meanings and purposes and leaves it to the reader to search them out for themselves. This process of diligently seeking out deeper meanings is vital, because pondering and querying helps one to understand the material better and decipher how it reflects the Logos Word of God, or His Spirit's revelation. Deep and diligent inquiry also separates the serious from the lighthearted and uncommitted and develops partnership with the Lord in His pro-creative Kingdom work.

The Bible exhorts us to seek, or diligently search, the Kingdom. Even in seemingly simple and familiar verses we find profound understanding. For example, "*In the beginning was the Word, and the Word was with God, and the Word was God*" (John 1:1) sounds simple but is actually loaded with profound truths. Books dealing with Kingdom eschatology, or last day kingdom theology, like Daniel, Isaiah, or the Revelation, are highly perplexing, and full of images. We are still required to search these out.

The poetry, songs, anthems, and mantra of a people are a condensation of larger worldviews. The poet, song writer, and philosopher, Pastor Grundtvig of Denmark, Robert Burns of Scotland, William Shakespeare, or even Sir Winston Churchill with his famous sayings, epitomized the soul, spirit, and aspirations of their nations. It is generally accepted that Pastor Grundtvig's works were important for the formulation of the modern Danish national consciousness. In his writings, he insisted that every Danish student know what would be termed "the poetry of Denmark."

Such nationally important poetry often includes topics and themes from every sector of the society, including areas like nature, love, romance and marriage, religion, entertainment, politics, and business. Many of these are absent from Christian literature, or thought of as taboo in some Christian circles. For this reason, this poetry book covers a wide range of the sectors of society, or "mountains of society."

One of the revelations of God in this generation is that the Lord is vitally interested in all these areas. He is interested that the last generation saints capture, manifest, and lead in all sectors of society (Isaiah 60:1–22). According to Isaiah 2:2 their worldviews are to be elevated and superlative above all the other "mountains of society"! Developing superior and divine wisdom in those areas starts from understanding and being involved in those areas. We are to appreciate the potentials, joys, pains, and contradictions contained in these areas. The Lord mandates us to invade these areas with divine wit. The Lord allows the author, through his various experiences, pleasant or nasty, to write passionately from the heart.

Regarding nature, for example, I start with the Bible position that the whole of creation groans and is equally aggrieved from the consequences of the original fall of man. It longs for the revelation and remedies from the sons of God regarding its numerous degradations. Interestingly, through quantum mechanics it is becoming apparent that inert objects respond to stimuli, even non-physical stimulus. In addition, by observing and experiencing nature and visiting various places, one is not only able to learn geography or history but "hear" what God is saying.

One societal issue often not written about in what can be termed "dry theological narrative" is love, romance, and marriage. Yet these topics are prevalent in the entertainment industry, and are the source of great social pain. They are often entry points for the enemy. King Solomon wrote His romance poetry not from a sensual angle but to truthfully spell out joys, pains, contradictions, and answers. In this book I pen a number of poems that talk of the sheer ecstasy of love but also of the pains, contradictions, and dilemmas common in finding true love and satisfying marriage, even in Christian circles.

Business and politics are other taboo areas in Christian circles. There is the traditional separation of state and religion, church mouse and secular affluence. Most Christians have abandoned these areas, and because of this void, the enemy has come in boldly and unchecked and has massively distorted these areas to his advantage and grand plan. The poem "Tell Your Brother" demonstrates how non-Christian politicians ridicule any Christian attempting to enter their jealously-guarded political and economic enclaves. The poems "North-South Dialogue" and "Palm oil Topping" portray the socio-economic tensions between developed nations and under- developed nations. The poems "Solar Line" and "Centrifugal Engine" demonstrate many African nations' political, economic, and social quagmires, and the bankruptcy generated by their own politicians' arrogance and exuberant living, a creation of both the Christian's apathy and absence in those areas. Ironically, right from the beginning of time the Lord has emphasized that the whole earth and every sector therein belongs to Him. Instead of us adapting to the secular and worldly systems, or giving up in despair, hoping only for a glorious eternity, the Lord wants His end time saints to be the ones to provide solutions and lead every currently confused sector.

The sections on religion, church, and faith provide a subtle yet firm theological understanding of who our God really is. In the poems "Cosmic Sergeant Major," "Wine Bibber," and "Melting Sun," for example, I provide a fresh but scripturally supported view of God, important for our true worship and understanding of our mandate. This points to our true origin and destiny in Christ. I also develop many poems reflecting the current position of the church. The poem "Avant-garde Morris" demonstrates the level of confusion and apostasy with the church. Similarly, the section on "Conflicts" demonstrates the general societal muddle and confusion. However, the poems "Foundations," "Aaronic Robes," and "Two Sips of Wine," for example, show that the Lord in this generation is bringing us to the correct foundations, faith, and purpose for the church in His Kingdom reign, hence providing direct solutions to various personal and societal alienations and contradictions.

ACKNOWLEDGEMENTS

I would like to thank my late parents, who not only passed on to me their literary and artistic genes, but also encouraged me from an early age to be interested in the creative arts. My father, Mr. Abuneri (Abner) Owor, a graduate of the famous Kings College Buddo, was for many years a school head, majoring in teaching history and fine art, then later a senior government administrator. My mother, Christine Owor, though not as well educated, was a spontaneous storyteller and composer of songs. She contributed to and was acknowledged in the first ever Acholi folk tale books by the late Professor Odonga. She also won many district competitions in cooking, home keeping, and community leadership.

I would also like to thank my school masters from the late 1960s: the head master of the Kabalega Secondary School, the late Mr. Peter Canham, and the Literature teacher of the same school, Martin Hill, who greatly encouraged me as I started my poetry writing. Later, during the same period, at Busoga College Mwiri, the school chaplain, Dr. Tim Kitwood, allowed me to compose gospel songs for the school chapel.

I would like to thank the following literature giants, who while at the University of Nairobi in the 1970s recognized that I was not a novice: Dr. Okot P'Bitek, Professor Taban Lo-liyong, and the late Professor Ambassador Dr. David Rubadiri, who helped me move beyond classical poetry writing. While at the Nairobi University, my peer, friend, and later the best man at my wedding, Professor Dr. Aloo Mojola Osotsi, who comes from a literature and philosophy background, not only taught me most of the techniques of poetry writing but gave me the challenge to write boldly on any subject.

I would like to thank Professor Chris Wanjala, who included my earlier poems in *Singing with the Night*, a book used in universities. He awarded me special mention in the very introduction of the book, where he said, "The Ugandan Silver Ocitti and Rugyendo are making their first appearance; but their verse is not un-masterly. Silver Ocitti blends myth with reality to explore the absurdity of man's situation."

While at the Edinburgh City Fellowship in the early 1980s, during my post graduate studies at the University of Edinburgh, my house group leader, Dr. Phil Moore, encouraged me to see poetry as an important part of Christian ministry. He read many of my poems at the Edinburgh church. My flat mate at the time, now a pastor and architect, David Hewitt, encouraged me to attend the performing arts Christian camp at Green Belt, England. Here, sitting in a workshop next to Sir Cliff Richard, I further discovered how ordinary, non-literary folk could deeply appreciate modern poetry as an important and relevant voice in their Christian lives.

If prophecy is not only foretelling but also forth telling the mind and heart of God, then I want to especially thank the following prophets, giants of our generation who through their writings have blessed me: Professor Dr. Vincent Anigbogo, a scientist, for declaring to us in his initiated "Institute for National Transformation, INT" how everything—creation, science, humanity—connect in God's eternal and grand plan. This further encouraged me to write on any topic boldly.

I'm thankful for the late Dr. Myles Munroe, who I believe through his years of study of the concept of "purpose" shed much light on the real purpose for the universal church. In my opinion, he also cracked the real understanding the Kingdom of God here on earth. Sunday Adelaja of the famous Ukraine church successfully demonstrated how that kingdom of God can operate and positively transform a nation.

To mention just a few more, I appreciate the following who, through their writing and forth-telling, greatly influenced my thinking on God's positive and practical plan for this last day generation and nations: Loren Cunningham, Neville Johnson, Steve Ogan, Kim Clement, and Chuck Missler. I also appreciate those writing not from the Christian point of view, but who in many ways reflect the mind and heartbeat of God by demonstrating that even in a seemingly dark and impossible personal and national situations, there is a way out. These include Lee Kuan Yiew, the first Prime Minister of Singapore; and motivational and business gurus like Jack Mo, Harv Ekker, and Napoleon Hill.

I am indebted to my wife, Harriet O'City, for her consistent prayers and for typing and re-typing many of the original manuscripts, and to my brother, Dr. Shannon Tito, in Canada, who after helping me publish my professional book in urban and regional planning, *Nucleated Villages*, together with Dr. Mojola insisted that these poems plus other books in the making be published not only for the local and regional readers, but for international consumption. I acknowledge Mr. Alex Mukulu, who in the early 2000s, allowed me to test-read some of my poems in the Uganda National Theatre, to much public applause! I'm also grateful to Professor Dr. Sam Siminyu for his guidance while previewing the first manuscripts of the sets of poetry some years ago. Thanks to Professor Taban Loliyoung, who after reading some of the completed works encouraged me to continue boldly in my creative manner and writing from the heart. I acknowledge Mr. Robert Kibuuka for giving me a valuable and detailed critique from a layman reader's point of view, of the final edited version of the first poetry book.

Last but not least, I'm grateful to my Lord and Saviour Jesus Christ and the Holy Spirit for giving these poems general direction and purpose to the last day church, especially the African church.

CONTENTS

OF NATURE

as green
as the original green,
and the blue sky;
mature,
with woolly clouds
that we love to paint
with Picasso
on our sun bunk beds.
Even mosquito bites
He created;
innocent-beautiful?

1. THE CHANGING SHAPE OF A CLOUD

a camel kneeling,
a reindeer poised
for a fight,
the map
of
India,
then
    three little
        rabbits
            that disappeared.

2. VICTORIA NILE

Roll on
Till you embrace
Your Egyptian dream;
Bathe Pharaoh's daughters
Hiding in the morning sun.
Farewell, you virgin molecules;
See you next time.
I fly over the Mediterranean.
Sail on, little Nile cabbages,
Sail on papering reeds;
Whispering reeds.
Hope you make it
Through the suds.
Foam on, skip
The Cushian granite;
One understands the excitement.
It's always a relief
Leaving the poverty line behind,
Bid blue-black skins,
And Stone Age Dinkas.
In fading coloured calicos,
Good-bye.
You carry presence,
Our treasured minerals
For their dying sands.
Hope they'll appreciate
Our little contribution
To their wheat silos.

3. MURCHISON FALLS NATIONAL PARK

absent liners   river gulls,   sorry antelope,
in distant baby-blue skies   their lazy songs. in the blue horizons,
                       await to be selected
                       to lunch a lion.

vulture circles
converting airs,
savanna green edges;   savanna green edges,
burnt-amber prairie.   a sin to miss.
         brown bucks,
loan sausage trees,   now seen, now not seen.
shade sleepy giants.   Burnt-amber prairie.
giraffe foot dents,   steaming-hot elephant dung hills.
Kobs dying to be counted.
          warthogs, foolish warthogs.   Birds from Sweden
                       perch here on their
                       abbatical.

NO HOOTING!   no driving after dusk.

bird watching on the Nile boat-launch   not yet decided which is better:
a one-time life experiences.   watching the falls from the top
                   or from the bottom;
                   my camera will decide.

leave wild flowers
for your grandchildren;   the entire Nile squeezes through a 13 feet canyon,
kindly.   at the Murchison fall's fall.
          Try that; you'll turn into mincemeat.

only elephants have the right to wear ivory,
crocs three metres long, one metre away;
don't elbow out of the boat.

       even if you are that excited, don't get out of the car;
       take pictures of a lioness feeding her cubs.

male antelopes with six hundred wives
—isn't fair

sumptuous buffet lunch bonfire African folk tales dreamt I was guide to
at the Sarova Hotel.   After-dusk-barbeque.   Sir Winston Churchill.
                                  at the Murchison Park.
                                  wish I could afford two more days.

another sumptuous buffet breakfast
at the lazy sunrise hotel terrace.

4. SMELL OF EDEN (BUDONGO FORESTS)

Luck.
I once flew
over the Budongo's
ancient greens; carpeted,
like bubbling moss,
to the Congo mother,
were one, once,
with savanna woods;
thinning, by nature,
by human amputation.
My wish,
like yours, to parachute, drop
pad land,
sinking into filtering greens
and fading sun
behind,
only for a walk
with butterflies,
flirt with man-like eyes,
only for a smell
of Eden again.

They say, "The more
beautiful the frog or spider,

the more lethal the venom."
So, twisting by vines
would be sure fun,
but get lost in her;
only compasses of luck,
will help see this ancient moss behind.

5. SSESE ISLANDS

Waiting for the Paradise baby
with leaves of unmocked liberation
to be born in the golden sun; in you,
Yet to see deeper greens
and swing in the lake winds;
breezes that cool molten hearts,
soothe concrete, and glass urban pains.

The chimney stacks are here,
Cough-fumes that condense
the acid rains are near.
If they gray the distant sky,
and the island rivers
that plate our candlelight
dinners and wine,
what is that to you?

But can we keep
the Ssese Parrot's
tunes of unmocked liberation,
their fluttering wings,
raiments of palaces,
beautiful in the wind?

Steel cultivators are here,
teeth that break dead sands
and lazy glades,

planted palm oil,
in military lines,
instead of Nkarati,
commanded to break march.
The gray trails are here;
rolling metals
that incise our citadels
with carbolic airs;
we fear they shamelessly
amputate mahogany giants,
leaving plastic glades, nude glades,
that swing and sway only
to locomotive music
on our coffin-sized balconies.
But the paradise parrots
hope against hope,
caged to our urban pergolas,
together mourn their reflections
and true-born dreams
of smiling tropical leaves dancing
to their songs of unmocked liberation.

OF PLACES

That touch your very navel

6. TABLE MOUNTAINS

You were so proud
Of your southern suns,
And your granular shores,
Yet to colour colourless.

You looked into the crystal ball
And saw that you would rule
Your brothers
With wrought iron prods.
Drove them into hellish pits,
To sieve dust from yellowing stones,
Made them fan
Your silver furnaces,
Just for the price of chicken wings.

Drunk Ceres juices
From your drunken valleys,
Where peaches grew
On black skin.
Drove them into hellish pits,
Made them sieve dust for Pentagon glass,
Made them dig pools,
Pools that blue your gardens,
And white mansions of Dutch Colonial.

You provoked your black brothers to anger
To lay their innocent black hands on machetes,
Spears, shot and long guns, shouting "Amanza!

Power to the people, power to the black brothers!"
You provoked God Himself,
Who created all equal, beautiful in His sight.
You provoked Him to anger;
In His wrath He severed off your head,
Circumcising the top off your pride.

Circumcised as you are,
You still look beautiful.

Cape Town, April 1993

7. MAN EATERS OF TSAVO.

Historical context: *The British colonial government in Kenya and Uganda brought cheap labour from the Gujarat region of India to work on the Uganda Railway through Kenya. When the construction reached the Tsavo region of south east Kenya, the crew encountered a pair of lions that hunted and killed many of the workers between March and December 1898. The lion's behaviour and the manner of the attacks was unusual. The story is well documented in the book <u>The Man-Eaters of Tsavo</u> by John Henry Patterson published in the UK by Macmillan and co, ltd in 1907. The majority of the Indian railway workers who survived the lions of Tsavo eventually settled in Kenya and Uganda after the Uganda Railway was completed. They started trading businesses and became very successful. Most of these former railway walker's and their descendants, however, maintained their British citizenship, even after living in Uganda and Kenya for several generations. Their wealth and lack of integration into Ugandan society frustrated the president of Uganda, Idi Amin. In August 1972, he expelled all members of the South Asian minority from Uganda, giving them only ninety days to leave the country. Most of them resettled in the UK and Canada, where they have continued to be successful in business.*

If it wasn't for the Uganda Railway,
Thank God,
If it wasn't for the Uganda Railway,
Snaking its way down the Rift Valley;
If it wasn't for my grandfather,
And the other Banianis from Gujarat,
Snaking the Uganda Railway
Through the Maasai savanna plains,
Feeding man-eaters of Tsavo
With their own flesh,
I would be like those Banianis,
Perched on the poverty side of the fence,
Watching us sip this Italian wine.

If it wasn't for Idi Amin,
Thank God Almighty,
If it wasn't for Idi Amin, now added
To yet another Gujarati god,
I wouldn't have this awesome mansion
In Hounslow Central,
Controlling humongous business lines
Worldwide.
If it wasn't for Idi Amin
Herding us off on the Uganda Railway,
To wherever the rail slippers hit the sea,
Stuffing some off on Uganda Airlines flights
To wherever the fuselage hit the sky,
We wouldn't be here,
Sampling this South Indian cuisine,
In this luxury Baroda Hotel.

Vadodara, India, July, 2002

8. WHEN I WAS IN SWITZERLAND

Thirty metres into Switzerland
Wasn't fair for my passport,
But thirty metres of a friendly gesture
Into fairytale-land was good for my friends.
Didn't see picture-framed Alpines and swan lakes,
With peaceful hamlets growing naturally;
Stop to lunch at Café Jean-Boulevard,
But thirty metres into Switzerland
Was good enough for my cocktail talk.

Italy-Switzerland border, September, 1998

9. THE THREE-LEGGED HAGGIS

Polished stone walls, slate roofs condensed in black hues, ecclesial spires
Competing in the mist, creatures padded in anoraks, head to toe, blow
    cold steam;
They brisk along, everything green, waiting till the next freezing summer.

Nicholson Street, the Royal Mile, Hay Market Street, Chambers Street,
    Baccleauch Street,
The names keep coming back, memories, serenity in solid, gray stone.

    I sketched the Queen Ferry Mew, every leaf,
    Every slate, every window.

                Went to take a Christmas card to
                my neighbour

On the way to Aberdeen, they said,   At 121 Dalkeith Road, he barked,
"If you look hard enough, you will see   "Aer you having a drink, mate?"
    I smiled,
The three-legged Haggis;   "I don't drink whisky; I don't drink alcohol."
A creature which flies backwards."   "Aer you a Moslem or are you what?"
                    "No sir," I said. "Orange juice will do."

"See that wuid? It's the door; Craig out of it!"
He shot after me.

Jogging in the snow was possible with thirteen chocolate bars a day.

David Hewitt said, "Instead of freezing here in these Pollock halls of residence,
Let's winter with these merry sledges on Arthur Seat mound.
See, even eighty-year old's slither with ease?"

Took me two whole months

Posed by my life-sized snowman;   To understand a word of Scottish;
Brilliant for my photo album   Pronounce Baccleuch

Soon, though, I could dribble the Glasgow thing: "Oaer you lookin at me or
aerr you chuin a brrick, cause either way you'rrre guin ti loose yourr teeth!"

Could even recite a few lines from Robert Burns' poems.

Appreciate now how you Scots are stone-willed; imagine lifting those stones,
Fashion the Edinburgh Castle, the Royal Festival Hall, at minus forty degrees.

That's why you become what you are when they whipped you
At the University of Edinburgh at minus forty degrees.

And so I lifted those books until the dean of the faculty called me aside
and said,
"Take it easy; you are doing all right. We bury at least one book every
year here."

The greatest British inventors and brains were Scots.
I am proud to be part Scot, from Kirl Kirde
North of Edinburgh, on forth of the firth—
Firth of the Forth.

Whenever I was homesick, I would stand by my window and look at the snow
over the Pentlands and pretend that was Got Kilak hills near Gulu.

Thank God, after twenty years away in the sun, I returned, just to look at the
    snow over the Pentlands again.

    Up to now, though, I am not convinced that
    The Loch Ness monster exists.
    By now it would have
    Posed with a *National Geographic* camera for a photo.

Walking along Princess Street on a Saturday afternoon is a once-in-a-life-
    time experience,
And in the park by the Royal Infirmary is what you need to think like
    Thomas Edison.

Walk around Arthur Seat; if you are lucky, you will meet the Duke of
    Edinburgh himself, Watching swans float on the Hollyrood Park loch.

Roll into those exquisite shops on Princess Street; they would brighten up at
    this rich, young Nigerian prince.
"Sorry, you don't seem to have a sixty-karat gold ring," I would smile out.

    You will be met by your new student's guide at the Waverly Station.
    I was looking for a place resembling the Kampala Railway station,
    With two nineteen canteen old, steam engines parked nearby.

Every summer, when the whole world converges on Edinburgh
To watch the castle burn,] and celebrate the goddess of the solar icicles,
I would be buried in my books, except for once. I watched a fringe play
At the Royal Mile. That was not at all funny.

At the 20 Chambers Street faculty, I can hear the blithely American
    Peter Block,
The non-skip Australian Annie Bryle, and the stupidly clever Tanzanian
    Faustin Kalabamu
Challenge our lecturer, Tim Birley, to a debate on Metropolitan swirl-soup
Or something equally acrimonious.

Best part was being part of the Edinburgh City Fellowship as a
Drummer in the church band; dribbled some tropical life on that iceberg.
And with the house cell group: Dr. Phil. Moore, Grandma Robby,
And the "Four Musketeers," David Hewitt, John Angus, Collin Symes,
    and myself.

I always looked forward to Scottish folk dance on New Year's Eve at the
Holly Corner's Hall. Still have my tartan Scottish kilt to this day, you bet.

I bought my first car in Edinburgh: Betsy, incredible piece of machinery,
a Datsun
One Hundred and Ten A.
The four musketeers would scuttle Scottish sisters every weekend in Betsy,
Looking for the three-legged creature that flies backwards.

Edinburgh, 1979 to 1981

10. ZERO CRANES

Care to join me tomorrow at the Taj Mahal?
It is Architecture in its purest form.
It's art, it's nacreous marble, untainted marvel;
It's perfect lines, perfect contours, perfect craft.
It is love extravagance; love wrapped in dill,
Romance marbled, romance marvelled.
It's a woman's penultimate dream,
To bury in Gold and to be buried in Gold.

Sorry, I would rather pen up here,
Take a walk around Connaught Place,
Whiz around downtown Delhi
In a happy-coloured rickshaw,
Before I can comprehend on whose backs
The Maharajah marvelled the marble.
Would be great to bury in dust gold,
Be buried in copious gold,

Confident of one's eternal animation.
But if in the life to come a moth you will be,
At best a temple monkey,
Then it is vanity of vanities.

I adore cunning craftsmanship, design articulation,
But I would love to know on whose backs
The lines were whipped into perfection,
And corner stones blood-sweat rolled into place;
Like Nile cranes lifting triangle stones.
Zero castes lifted Taj marbles with zero cranes.

New Delhi, India, November, 1999

11. MYRIAD SIGHTS

The best sight: a centrifugal circle or T-junction,
Where all laws and non-laws of motion converge;
Motion in perfect harmony, perfect mayhem?
Elephants, Horses, Mules, Deity Cows, Stray Hounds,
Exploding flights of aimless Pigeons,
None stripping, none crippling, none bickering.
Rickshaw, Tricycles, Bicycles, Motorcycles,
In full speed, in full steam, loaded full brim.
Vans, Prams, Buses, Lorries, Cars, and Carts,
All have learnt to co-run with each other,
At the merry go round, round-about,
In perfectly controlled oriental disorder,
In time-honoured, totally organized chaos.

Land of intoxicating, myriad, melodramatic sights;
Verandah scums, medium rich dukawalas, super rich bellies,
Weave pass each other, none stepping on each other's toes
Lest they are buffed, puffed, a floating corpse on the Ganges.
Dhal making, hand-wafted furnaces, nuclear technology;
They can even chip a microchip, seated on hand-woven sisal mat.

Charge you one-eightieth, the one from Silicon Valley;
Chips that look like Tata Lorries but can last ten times longer.
Went to a discreet garment factory making discreet shirts for Harrods
     of London,
Looked at the colours, on them were written: Made in England.

Beef Vindaloo, Pork Balchao, Misi Rotis, Parathas, practically any Parathas,
Curries so hot your tongue won't distinguish between mutton curry and
     chicken curry.
I shied away from the roadside cafes, went safe to the five-star hotel;
Had the worst diarrhea, my kiosk-food-eating friend giggling away.
Cardboard slums, honeycomb apartments, marble castles,
So long as you pay the rent for at least one night, and off you go.
Paddy fields, tiger forests, monsoon palm trees, temperate trappings,
Snowcapped turbans, sand capped dunes, yellow capped plains:
You can see it all, seated no-class, on the roof of any north-south train.
Yellow-Ochre skin, like most, white skins, whiter than the Alps;
Black skins, must be Luos left behind from the Second World War.
Masters, slaves, total slaves, total thieves, especially at railway stations;
Untouchables, total rags, temple prostitutes, what more can I say?

Squares, homos, half men, half women,
Hermaphrodites: can pay to see one.
Hindus, Buddhists, Moslems, Catholics,
Gods, humans, temple monkeys,
In perfect harmony, accepting human dictum, declaring no encumbrance,
Ignoring divine destiny, applied grace, declaring no reticence.
None stripping, none crippling, none bickering,
Land of intoxicating, myriad, chromatic sights.

Mumbai, November, 1999

113. BAR-EL-GAZEL RANCHES

Ladies and Gentlemen, we are now entering the South Sudan air space.
To the right of the fuselage is the new and remolded border town of Kapueta.
It controls and monitors the exit of every diamond chip, like gates to
    the Pentagon.
In the past, teak timber, gold, croc skin, even crude oil from Aweil,
Did promenade out like un-mortified whores, parading in a Sherrie daylight.
To your right one can witness savanna-span corn fields and wheat fields,
Stretching as far as the eye blacks out and the yellow ochre fades into the blue.
Some obdurate minister was playing a Monopoly game with Americans
    and Japanese,
In who offers him better apartments in their cities, and roll for him tank-
    like cars,
Just to give them monopoly and manifold control over this vast granary.
But thank God for our God-fearing president, who discovered Africa's
    last riddle.
He said, "Any minister caught battering away Sudan soil would be thrown in
    the Nile,
Eaten by Juba crocodiles, his family watching, the cabinet singing the
    national anthem."

To the left one can see a vacuum land, every square inch loaded not with
    corn ears
But Uranium, Platinum, Tanzanite, Tantalite, Sudanite and other form
    of nites.
Below us a modern settlement, three thousand such so far across the South,
Modelled after the Lutuku Manyattas, or English hamlets, built from scratch,
Each complete with housing, schools, health centres, shopping malls.
One can see modern co-operative farms mindfully prearranged, displayed.
They market their produce to cottage industries, in which they too have shares.
No grain, no leaf, leaves the settlement or region unprocessed, in raw form.
Don't be surprised if some of the food you have eaten on board came
    from here.

Ah! On your right is a monument erected where the great founder of
    this nation,
The late Dr. John Garang, met his death in a helicopter crash; it is now a
    tourist site.
To the left and right again, more farm land, the citrus and grape home of
    the world.

Now we take a deliberate detour; to access Juba from Yei mango town,
To give you a totally different landscape, we have been over the tropical
    savanna plains.
Now we'll show you the deep green moss of tropical forest and leafy
    elephant grass,
Where mangoes grow wild, though some say they are trails of Arab
    slave traders.
But now the mangoes are harvested and bottled, and bananas for the
    European market.
You see there on your immediate right one such juice and jam process-
    ing plants.
Southern Sudan has six of such geographic, ecological zones; we have just
    seen two.
Would take us three whole days knotting at this speed and flying this low to
    view all.
You have, for example, the Lake District, rich black Dinka dairy farms, and
    fish ponds,
You have Bar-el-Gazel ranches, worth stopping there for ardent meat eaters
    on board.
You see that forest, it stretches to its Congo mother, its pure natural teak, old
    as Adam.

Now Ladies and Gentlemen, may you kindly fasten your seat belts as we
    embark on
Our descent into Juba, new Juba actually, since it was pointless remodelling
    the old.
As the good book says, you can't put new wine into old wineskin, lest
    both explode.

In many ways the New Sudan had to come to major departure with the old
dress code,
The old mentalities, old economic school, traditional non-Son ethos, embraces
the new.
You can see New Juba, as modern as any in the world, so you need not
fear pick-pockets,
No one with an Arab dagger, we no longer follow the sharia law.
In case you are staying in Juba for a while, the captain and the entire crew says
"Bier Thuon Deng."

South Sudan, 2011 onwards

114. DATE-PALM OASIS

You need to relocate your brain cells to take a visit to Dubai, sing its
desert song.
Surrender your town's soul tie, be it New York, Georges Town, Nairobi,
or Canberra.
Forget the name of your mayor for a while, his attempt to rekindle his foren-
sic town.
Possess this new bride, romance her, but shift your brain to celebrate a visit
to Dubai.
You need, though, purses and purses, even in Sharjah: Dollars, Francs,
Yens, whichever.

To gloat the malls, complete with desert ice skating rinks, predict marble-
glazed precincts
Of Italian cunningness, Malaysian cane, and Japanese electricity, you need
those Dollars.
To say you are penniless is a disgrace to your national flag and wife back
at home.
Simply float your nose across food courts, everything Thai to Mexican
cuisine, cheaply,
And forget the air-burgers that filled your lunch shame-bag back home.
What alibi to your good lady, evading the Dubai Gold Market, Hand Bag
World Show?

Baffling how these Arabs keep their white robes white with so much Ramadan
    food to eat.
Didn't see many mosques, temples. It's business, pleasure, skyscrapers,
    and technology,
And the pursuit for more business, pleasure, skyscrapers, and technology.
The older folk thank the good Lord, even in their parliaments, on their
    national days,
For lifting them out of the date-palm oasis, trading them out of desert
    arm bushes.
The young breeze in their latest model Japanese models, all night, with their
    unveiled girls.

The best part still is to shoot one's self up the new Babel tower, with clouds
    below you,
Taking a vantage viewpoint of this beautiful world,
But beware of talking tall like that Babel tower talk, lest the owner of the
    clouds say,
"Enough of this pensive pride, back to the desert, back to camel humps."
Once you compete with His deferential angels, your floors in the sky have
    no altitude.

At the Burj-al-Arab, for once, you pen with the famous, rich and favoured of
    the world;
Good thing is, so long as you can pull out them dollars, no one requires your
    voter's card,
And so, to sample the best of French Meringue Torte and Signature
    Italian Pistachio
At the helipad, without any security uniform infuriating you, "Sign
    here, please."
If you are an Architect like me, and like sketching every pole, you have
    my sympathy;
Your dreams will be exploding silhouettes, intoxicating glass memories,
    and palm-sea.
Out into the sea: man-made islands, world architects compete to sketch
    their brains,

For architectonic architecture, new forms, shapes that thrill not only the sheiks
But even holidaying millionaires from metropolitan London and proud-tall
    New York.

In Dubai, every Dollar a welcomed friend to the tent but insists you rename
    it Dirham,
Paint every cunning imagination but insist you embrace an Emirate as partner.
But you will return home agreeing, "A city is not merely an intoxicating
    concrete form,
A pinnacle that touches the clouds, a whore that calls trading ships to port,
But an imagination, how to turn anything you have in your hands to
    a commodity
That calls trading ships to port, midwifes a parched sand to produce green,
    crispy lettuce.

115. LAMBORGHINI SUEDES

It's
Ferrari,
Marennello,
Lamborghini suedes,
Michelangelo,
Leonardo da Vinci,
Italian wine,
Etched glass,
Stainless steel,
It's art domesticated:
Creativity at its best.

It's
Marble nudes,
Spitting gargoyles,
Happy demi-gods,
Italian wine,
Over-fed pastas,
Private helipads,

Two-day governments,
Mafia money,
It's the Vatican in control.

It's Tourist churches,
And more Tourist churches,
No one saying Amen,
Clicking cameras,
Enunciating,
"Gloria in excelsis."
Confessed sins
Recovered,
At the quadrangle.
It's Italian wine,
Brawly beggars,
Coin.

It's
Pompeii grills,
Moldy clay tiles,
Italian wine,
Wrinkled landscape
Begging to retire,
History dying
To be remembered,
The new,
Competing to be forgotten.

Millan, November, 1993

116. ZANZIBAR

I only stopped at the gray-haired airport transit lounge,
Didn't go into the old Arab town, mangrove creeks.
Would have loved a visit to the Sultan's guilt-wash castle,
Elope with a five-star, hand-carved wood hotel,
Discuss spices to slave trade, brave the Sultan exit talk,
Pour elongating coffee from Moroccan copper jars;
Cashew nut, and coconut cookies in plenty,
Swaddle in bed-like chairs, and chair-like beds.
But then I only stopped at the airport transit lounge.

I would have loved to coble and pave stone alleys,
Feel the arched catwalk fly-overs, peep windows,
Nun-veiled women gossiping sins by the alcoves.
I would have loved to trace the random tourist-type stops,
Overstuffed cinnamon kiosks; emerge knick-knacked,
Take pictures with paw-paw fresh, smiling school kids;
Off springs of Arab-African condominium living.
I would have loved to practice my coastal Swahili
At the corner cafes, and drink over sweetened tea
Poured in piping hot glasses with oily cinnamon mandazis.
But then I stayed back at the airport transit lounge,
Taking flat continental airport left-luggage tea
Pelted out in economy class plastic tupperware.

I love the African clutter market, at par with its organized chaos,
Women in tropical Kitenges, and humane Swahili men
Vending ebony wood carvings, naïve art, spice gift bags,
Carts full of coconut milk, sunk straight from the load.
I would have loved to accept a typical Zanzibar Karibuni-welcome;
To a Makuti, mangrove pole roof, Coral stone bungalow,
That hides and seeks among sky-high coconut trees,
Gladden to a chilled mango juice and barbequed lemon-fish,
Oblivious Kanzu men playing the African pebble chess,

And lazy peacocks patrolling the clove grooves;
The smell of sea water-fish, the smell of the day.
But then I stayed back at the airport transit lounge,
Taking flat continental airport left-luggage tea
Pelted out in economy class plastic tupperware.

Zanzibar, July, 2003

117. RIVERS OF BLOOD-GUILT.

I visited Kigali, Rwanda in 1994, just after the famous Rwanda genocide. The testimonies of some is that the organizations that saw it coming, or had the ability to prevent it, just stood silent, watching the butchering. Some of these could have had a part in the breeding of the discrimination.

I saw death
walking
the streets of Kigali,
and rivers of blood-guilt
flowing,
and I asked,
"Why are there no more demons
in hell,
now all on the streets of Kigali,
and who will atone
this blood bath?"
then came a French catholic nun's riposte,
"Maybe the Tutsis,
maybe the Hutus."

Kigali, November, 1994

118. HAY MARKET (EDINBURGH)

will walk
      your cobbled street
            AGAIN

Edinburgh, November 2002

119. CLIFFS OF MOHER

To the Left,
You stretched,
Rifling brewed cream;
To the Right,
You vanished,
Into billowing mists.
I threw a stone;
It searched
Your bottomless pit;
Like gravity,
It searched.
Out in the sea,
A gull perched
From the land
Of painless bliss.
But there I was, still,
Standing helplessly
On the Cliffs of Mother.

The Republic of Ireland, July 1980

120. **THE COLOSSEUM**

I remember you still,
Through my Hiroshima camera;
With overfed Manhattan sausages,
Clicking this and clicking that,
Every casual jean agreeing,
"Magnificent, magnificent."

I could still hear
The piteous, unsung heroes,
My brethren, moan and wail,
As the sea of people squeal,
Cubs mauling their ball.

Abeyance, Abeyance.
Impressed, you stand
Your rickety ground,
Everyone clicking this,
Everyone clicking that,
At the stones.

Hear the comfort call:
"Take courage;
It won't be long."

Rome, December, 1993

121. OLIVE OIL TO MY VEGETABLE SALAD

From the Hotel Ivanhoe,
Can one see the Vatican City?
Then I poured more olive oil
To my hollow salad plate ...
Did the Romans also have so much pasta?

Yes, of course!
More wine, mate,
Flows here like water---

No thanks,
I don't drink.

Are you a Moslem?
Yes, from the Hotel Ivanhoe,
You can't see the Vatican City.
That too,
Is my problem.

Rome, November1993

122. NEW RAND TALK

Zimbali, Four Square, Santon City, Waterfall Estate, any satellite towns,
Circling abandoned inner-city broods, sighs of relief, fears eased?
New names, new synergy, argued from every compass point,
New metropolitan sprout or neo-apartheid; built to last?
You look beautiful to me, architectured Dutch-colonial and more,
Clean, pure, litter free, no lazy bones roam malls, brisker strides,
Far from the maddening crowd, from knifed street corners.
New mix, all colours welcomed: white, red, green, black;
Upper middle class and above, simply complete the mortgage,
Best still, pay cash, plagiarized or gold slid grandfather to grandson,
The difference is the same; meet you in the hood; at the club.

Just learn to say "Hi!" at the gate, at the school's parents' day.
Be on the same page, when Rand talk is sipped at the club,
And the new South Africa prepares for another holocaust?

South Africa, March, 2007

OF LOVE

like his
conflicting romance;
his love,
and the sex
that awaits true green.
His marriage
endures.

6. PRAIRIE DREAM

always dream
of romancing with you
on a golden-brown prairie field,
with the sky as blue
as a kindergarten blue,
and convecting eagles
singing our love song.

always dream
of running through corn ears
with you,
with you cheeky
as a high school calf;
your floral skirt
sailing in the autumn breeze,
even when we taper off our prairie race
it sails still.

But then
the picnic basket must wait
till we are full
of our love song.

7. WRONG BONE

Where were you
At Cupid's parade,
At the beauty line,
And the cat-walk test
For soft hearts?

It couldn't be you;
I couldn't see you,
When my pillow needed
A suave flesh,
Yardley aroma,
When God
Molded a mate
And sighed,
"As for you,
A rib much fairer.
A rib less fair
Would do you harm."

8. THIS TIME

this time,
it must be you;
this time, it must be it.

lavender butterflies flutter
your favourite colours;
green lily blades sway
with wings of spring.
this time, it must be God;
peace;
a throbbing striving heart ceased.

this time, angels dancing

On multi-coloured raindrops.

listen, church bells ringing,
and bubbles of love-hearts
fill the air.

9. SONG TO MY LOVE-EYES

lie here,
on my lap.
it is soft;
softer than pillows
of cloud,
and together,
you and I,
we'll make
the moon smile.

arose;
one of its petals fell
on your chiffon dress,
and we both agreed
it did well.

tell me
once again,
how your limbs turned into rubber
the day you first saw me.

or do words
fail you now,
then let it be enough,
just to hear
the sound
of your heartbeat
dance to my love-eyes.

10. **BEHIND**

oh yes,
what was
the name
of the girl
from Fort Hall?
imagine me say,
"oh yes,
what was the name
of the girl
from Fort Hall?"

11. **BONI'S GIRL**

The time
we first kissed,
the moon had
stolen a nap
behind the sailing clouds.
The last choir member
had just wheeled off
into the mist.
I could hear
the security man
pace the church compound,
and she said,
"Imagine!"

12. **FIRST COFFEE**

Not even a smack on her cheeks
Had I to do it all over again,
Before her first organ step,
An unregenerate finger float
Her chintz innocuous frock.

Had I to do it all over again,
Only upon her opal eyes I would,
With love shades that conceal
One's obstinate blood pressure;
Was glad I kept on the buttons.

Had I to do it all over again,
Would even request her father,
Date our first coffee,
And if he blurts, barks out,
I would regret an omission malady
Requesting the Father, our first coffee.

13. **SAHARAH BODY**

Your curves
are sand dunes
to me;
perfect
to my hands,
nipple stopped.

14. **MORE BISCUITS**

*After returning to Kenya, from my studies in the UK, in 1982, I eagerly went
to visit one of my girlfriends, hoping the friendship could turn into a marriage.
Her mother, knowing my reason for the visit, had the uncomfortable task to tell
me that the lady had already been married and had moved with the husband to
Paris!*

how many sugars ...
Rose told me you'd gone
to study in Britain.
it's been a long time indeed.
by the way,
Rose now lives
with her husband in Paris.
more biscuits please ...
sorry I have to leave;
there's a Mother's Bible Study
at church.

15. **AT THE ALTAR**

suffice it
young man.
you have kissed
her veil
as well!

16. **LAST STEP**

She chewed me
her story,
from the time
the waiter curtsied,
"Table for two?"
to the time

he bowed,
"Don't forget your umbrellas please,
Sir,
that was quite a story ...
Mind the steps!"

17. HEART-LONG FALL

Was close to a fall into a highland loch,
Close to dipping my numbed brain cells,
Break frigid surface tension; wooing ripples,
Contemplating this gal from Aberdeen.
Tumbling, to the deep end, following too,
Heart-long into this dumb black sheep;
Her Hebrides charm beyond Mona Scottish.

Alas sagacity wrapped, a firth wind wrap,
Divine astuteness alone queried the din-gain
Of a one Aberdeen gal, speaking softly,
With me standing; me a refugee, evacuee emaciated,
Floating with the wind, citizen of dust land.

On being pounced, pronounced, promulgated,
A Master of Philosophy Highland Haggis,
From the University of Edinburgh,
Three grace days extended, settle caution monies,
Clear arrears with late baked bean shops,
Out of the Isles; you are out, by Gibraltar boat
Or any bird that flies to the Equator.

So sagacity visited me again, harder,
"Look upwards into your own, brain cells,
Than caress a bleating, beating heart.
Appertain a Master of Philosophy Highland Haggis."

18. ORGANZA EYES

When we first melted
In the restaurant cabin,
On the night train
To Mombasa,
I laid this heart,
"Wouldn't it be affluent
We were all hermaphrodites,
Then I would rest my gaze
Into your Organza lenses;
Stabled, favourless.
Rather be petrified
By my unloading laptop.
And she smiled, "But God knew."

19. HEIGHTENED DESTINY

Fingernail varnishing queens perched to marble vanities,
Gaze hours at their eyelashes, admire the powdered tones.
Used to fans; deities that nibble, tenderly, Crème de menthe slices,
Fondle delicately minuscule, gold-rimmed porcelain.
With tea-like duchess and baronesses, discussing amakihi nectar.
Now I wonder, without adeptness, the eyelashes keep house,
Without proficiency, of un-sore fingered chamberlains,
How finger queens keep homes ripe with rector-linear teens, in-
    house grannies.
Fair to dawdle on pedicure, manicure, and other feminine cures,
Linger on the pergola terraces, gloss digested mode magazines.
But will she keep house with rector-linear teens, nieces, in-house grannies?

When the going is excellent, it is sail on silver lake and smiles parade,
When inactivity reports bank alerts, red flashes on the ATM screens,
Will vestibule porches smile, "May I handle your coat, please?"
When the credit card is punctured, bills perched on the roof ridges,
Will the sailing slide unforced, butter-smooth and shopping done in-flight?

Will she bend face the "Bend-low" happy air markets, jump muddy ditches?
The house helps will, but never night it a baby's convulsions night,
Serve the master orange juice in bed she may, but at some womanness loss.
It is vogue to walk, waist angled this way, fingers angled that way,
But will she culminate a generation breeder, help-meet him pioneer
Where the running water is rapid waters alone,
Electricity thunderbolts, and still bake the kids their birthday cake?
Will she soil vegetables, herb patch, or wait it straight from the can?

Who flags not a hip a la mode, marble lit malls, boutiques begging,
Banqueting with the town's clockworks, and other crème de menthes?
Who fancies not a lazy Bali bed, with sand, sea, and palm trees marry-
    ing easily?
But if you have to go through the testing, pruning, lose a few leaves,
As the Negro spiritual breathes it, "Into each life some rain must fall,"
Will she run back to shelter, warm and dry, unattained destiny heightened?
To reach destiny heightened, Paul apostles it,
"I've learnt to dawdle in six-star saloons and to creep in half pit lodges."

20. WHO CARES?

Who cares   In public,
Her slip   At times
Creeps,   It peeps?

Who cares   Doesn't yours
She knocked   Sometimes?
The Sunday roast,

Mortified
Guests pelting,   We'll roast
                  Many more roasts,
                  Sundays after.

    Who cares?
She can't replace
A burnt-out fuse,

You try that,
With the smell of garlic
Up your nose,
And the baby gurgling
In the cot.

This is deep bone-marrow talk.

Who cares,

Forsaken
The Seventh-day
Adventist handbook
On flesh-free plates.

She is now
Mother to my
Three little kids
To me too,
Guardian angel.

Begun to
Resemble
Flattened curves

And the bachelors
Wished they had cared.

She's Love
In one word,

Pronounce
Misappropriation,

She's now
flesh of my flesh
And my bone marrow too.

Try a diet:
Dill water,
Celery,
Macadamia nuts,
And raw mushrooms,
To keep up the vogue.

Layers upon layers
Of mayonnaise
On succulent duck cubes,
Golden brown Corn
Rolled in.

Who cares?

Will never forget
The day
The church bells
Aisled her come.

I mean,
Who cares?

21. LOVE TRAP

Flavia,   My first love,
                    You left without a mark
                    On your cheeks.

Margaret,   Married and moved.

Ray-x,   Rachael,
I used to call   I said, "How come
You Ray-x,   You are so beautiful?"
                           And you said,
                           "I don't know."

Sarah,   Where did I go wrong?

Kate,   How far,
                           How long
                           Does one chase a butterfly?
Loving you   June.
Was as like one bad dream;

Janet,   Is this it,
                            Or yet another romance trap?

Anita   It's not your spirit level;
At least you did not   It's not your face level;
Hide behind some spiritual alibi.   It's your purse level,
                           Moreover, from area Z-X.

Then I said,   From area Z-X
                           We say,
                           "He who denies you
                           The delicious *Odi Ngwen*
                           Has saved you from diarrhea."

22. **SOBERING FACE**

I searched
For a sobering face,
A neutralizing ace.

Awhile I lingered,
Among blank,
Bouncing dates;
Were beautiful,
But,
Like leafing bitter herbs,
I regretted my sin.

I wasted my years
Jumping
From nurse to nurse,
Looking for a sobering face,
And He said,
"When you are through,
Please give me a call."

Didn't take another dice
Before I saw ...
I was indeed a beat-up case.
Then He said,
"Lie down here,
On my anesthesia bed,
And I will rib you
A woman fit,
Just for you."

23. **KIND CURVES**

She walks
Like a Crested Crane;

She walks.
She loves
Like LOVE;
Her love.
She's kind,
Like Mother Teresa;
My bet.
Her head
Is decked
On beautiful curves.
That's my wife.

24. **OVER TO YOU**

Thing is,
The Almighty has
Privileged us men,
Priority Choice,
Pick our own wives.
But if you own up,
"Sir, even that I've miscarried
Over to you."
Then believe you me,
He will fashion for you
A creature, crafted, hewn
Direct from Grace's throne;
Believe you me,
A wonder after God's own heart,
A worship leader,
Generation breeder,
A beauty mirror,
Mirrored to Proverbs 31,
Just like my wife.

25. JUST A FEELING

Had I married Patricia,
Sheepishly I would be aproned;
Cooking in turns,
As in a Scout's jamboree camp.
Now I cook when I cook,
And the kids,
Even my burnt Scottish Egg-burgers,
They've named it "Scorched Burger-Egg."

Had I married Jupiter Eyes,
The gal we used to call Jupiter Eyes,
I would be as worried
As a man with a cat-walk lady:
Look at Abraham's Sarah,
Look at Jacob's Rachael,
Look at Queen Vashti.
They say the more Jupiter the eyes,
The more hell the eyes.

"That one would give you
As much stick
As she would give you joy,"
Warned my friend Taki.
So I steered clean of Julie;
Her Saturday shopping basket,
A twenty-foot container,
Enough for a church retreat basket.

Had I married Jean,
I would be jumping college mews
In my blue don-jean,
Looking like a textbook,
Just for the sake
Of ending that academic robe,

Become her World Bank Rep. dream.
But then I said,
"Enough chalk is enough chalk."

Had I married Robinah,
I would be in the States by now,
Chasing some wild American dream.
But then I said,
"Rather be a millionaire in the Congo,
Than a million Coca-Cola cans
In America."

Had I married
The girl we used to call "Bitter Sweet,"
I would still be listening
To her chewing-gum talk,
Arguing on some useless gum,
Turning my living room
Into a university staff room.

Just a feeling:
Had I married the "Sizzler,"
I would be wondering whether
Our sex life was normal,
Properly adjusted,
Or whether we were living
By the blues that come
On the telly after ten.
Definitely,
I would be on my knees
In the Pastor's vestry,
Trying to save
The eighteen-karat gold.

Some pick theirs like grafted mangoes,
Others search among prayers and fasting;
Even so, some through agonizing groans.
"Important thing,"
My friend Mojola would say,
"Is to receive
Whoever the good Lord has ordained
For your ugly face."

26. REMAIN ENDED

Remain ended,
Prayed up,
And you will end up
With whoever
You will end up
To the end.

27. EASY CAT-WALK

Would glint dreaming of you, night after night, fashioning a jubilee walk,
And grin wider grins than leers that mellow lenses and plastic cheers.
Need I day-talk with you more; non-talks, evaporated easily,
Lunch with you more; prawns only, at the easy-walk restaurant,
Maybe sport with you more; brain soft Ludos game, that's all,
Sing with you quaint ballads, a love gift of red pomegranates,
Maybe join in the circles of kids in their silly love songs.
My guess, would they not surpass a call to a heartless company ball?

From suspended patios we watched lazy sails on silver lake drift lazy lovers;
We swaddled, poked crackling coals alone, in a love-shaped cottage,
Laughed at our baby's first gravity free walk, our lone Christmas Eve.
My heart has now tutored, repented of evaded lunch dates.
Love consummated like military drills is love blended amiss.
So came the evaporated non-talks at the easy-walk restaurant.

OF GOD

like the God
who walked
the botanical beaches
of Eden,
is now
like the God
who will be

28. WINE BIBBER

In Pubs,
They say,
And sin places,
A glutton; wine bibber.
Prostitutes
Become friends,
And tax collectors dine ...
Nicer than God
Saints of today
Stumble.

Play hide and seek
With little girls
And little boys;
Play,
Easy kingdom game.

Crude,
Undiplomatically direct,
Challenge your board
Of deacons
To a game of chess,

Hold Sunday services
On Wednesday
If you dare;
Radically think.

Incredibly plain,
Unstately,
Appearing obscure,
God,
We need your help.

Nazareth;
Extraordinarily degrading,
Geographically zero
On the maps,
A carpenter;
Hung his sign,
"WE MAKE BETTER YOKES."
Joseph and Sons
Limited,
By trade and space.
You are the last person
I'd predict
As Messiah sent.

Politically unconvincing,
Mysteriously evading,
A King without a car or army,
Zechariah's son up in rage.

But
I see now, you Adolf,
The obedience
Of more men
Than our friend Hitler,

Rule
In the hearts
Of your lovers;
The lame begin to walk.
Don't you see?

Your church,
Despised of men,
True,
But line the bottom,
You are bringing in
The rule of God
In the earth;
An army,
Marching through the land,
Saving hearts, Nations,
Proclaiming
The salvation of the Lord.

29. THE MELTING SUN

A is for Alfa.
Bridegroom; born
In Bethlehem,
Bigger brother,
Best.
C is for Christ;
Crucified, Caesared,
Conquered death,
Crossed the death line clean.

D is for David's son,
Is for Dayspring;
The tender mercies
Of the Father shining,
Hope to them that

In darkness sit, dazed.

Emmanuel—E;
With us was God,
Is still,
First born of the Father.

Good shepherd,
God;
Himself God,
Higher than any height,
Is for the High priest,
Above all heads,
Be in church or State.

Invisible King;
Visible only
To the hearts
Who know Him.

Jesus, Jesus;
The name
Above all names,
King of Kings,
Lord of Lords,
Master, Messiah anointed,
Bright Morning star.

They called him
A man-made son
From Nazareth;
Nil on the maps.

Omega, Omni-present,
Ombudsman.

The end of all things.
Will remain when all things present
Will un-present themselves
In the melting sun.

P
Is for our Passover sacrifice,
Is for Prince of Peace,
But for Satan
And his panting demons,
A Paralyzing Power.

Quint;
Is for thirst questner,
Quickener,
Giving life
To all men,
Whether in pews
Or in tombs.

Rider in the sky,
ROO 33 AD,
Identified flying object,
Resurrected.

Saviour—S;
Sure Son
Who crossed our sin
With a shout.

T is for teacher,
Truth;
Of the way
And the life.

Unchanging
Unlike U and me,
Who loved the world
And gave himself for her;
Like a lover.

Victor is for venom
Over Satan and the vices
Of its various demons.
The Vine who
Is our LIFELINE supply.

The word born
Was good;
Good news to all men.

Exalted;
We exalt
Him exceedingly,
Above all things.

X-mas
Is not for the
Oven-golden-brown bird,
With cranberry sauce,
And the minced meat tea
We enjoy so much,
With white-bearded Santa
Wishing every miserable sinner
A drunk and merry Christmas.

But x-mas is for Christ,
And Christ is for x-mas,
And Christ alone.

Y is for
Yesu,
Mukama wange,
The same in Africa,
Indonesia, or North America.

Z
All things
Will zero down
In his eternal reign,
Completed by him,
With him, and for him,
At his zest coming again.

30. COSMIC SERGEANT MAJOR

You curled me easy, Sergeant Major,
Saw your sadistic eye
Scanning this humble earth,
Freeze a giggling heart.
Heard you whipped out Wall Street
From a Jewish temple—was fair.
Wonder, though, your sanction,
That Nordic Claus that must
Reward every insidious brat,
Every sludge wintry night.

Were you being the nebulous prince,
Living in a lemon curd palace?
What use were you, what gain,
To a working-class Jews,
Unending wars, African scum,
Famine amidst buried diamond?

Last night I dreamt you were
The unidentified flying object
Of the *Star Wars* saga,
Booked you for an Oscar Award;
It tickled my mind.

Searched you still, enquired
Among ecclesiastical stone for grace;
Oh, for redemption of this sin-sick soul.
Stared at the ancient glass; stained beautiful,
Just for a solace, supple word.
All could hear was altar bells
In Latin, ringing, "Angus Dei, Angus Dei."

Sadness beyond sadness; tears ...
My aching soul buoyed on the devil's lake.
Slowly then searched the Milky Way for truth,
Folded my limbs in Buddha.
Determined now, only for a suspended bliss
Of Nirvana, may thin myself through
Eternity's keyhole, soothe sin-ulcers.
Contemplating further my bottoms
Flush with a bed of Eastern nails,
Indulge peace for my soul.

Then soft, the truth it came,
"Tonight, if you believe, you can
Spare your bottoms the Eastern pains.
I am not that Cosmic Sergeant Major,
But a loving father who has paid it all.
I reside in a divine penthouse, a tycoon,
Have Rockefeller on my payroll,
Truly so a nebulous prince
Among the scum of the earth.

Inter-planetary astronauts are
For Vandenikel's paperback, cheaply,
Fairy tales are for children of school;
I am the Great I am
For you to give your worshipful love.

See how I taught and lived?
A real time-space man.
Search me not in ancient stone,
Lakes, stars, or in the upward milk.
In spirit, truly, only worship."

31. SOUND OF MANY WATERS

Look!
He looks
A man.
Despised,
Abused.

Kagu
Maka
Kareba.
Look!
His hands,
His feet,
His side;
Pierced
For me;
A body
Bruised,
Just
For me.
What a faith,
A friend,
Love.

Day one
Died,
Day two
Loved,
Day three
Arose.
Now sits,
Angels
Around.
See
How
He looks;
A Son
Of
God.

Kareba.
Look
At
His face!
Shines;
A
Noonday
Sun.
Son.
Look!
His feet;
Made
Of gold,
Pure;
Pure gold.

Kagumakareba.
Look!
His hair,

White
As wool,
Soft
As wool.
Look!
At
His eyes;
Piercing.
Hear
His voice;
Sounds
Of thunder,
Sounds
Of waters.

Give
Him
Your praise,
All.
He's worthy
To be
Worthy,
To be praised.

32. WAS SACCHARINE

Syrup
From the sugar cane
Was sweet,
Was saccharine,
Sweeter than
Bee-honey.
It tastes
    Sweeter.

It's high;
It's altitude,
Higher than all heights
Can be.
Height
Isn't What
You see;
    Higher.

It's bright;
It's light;
It shines through
The darkest hour,
Piercing
Through
Sin,
I see;
    Brighter.

It's sharp;
Be careful,
A two-edged sword,
Now
Zapping through
Spirit and soul;
    Sharper.

Rapa Daba,
Rapa rapa Daba,
Rapa Daba,
Rapa rapa Daba,
That's what it is,
Rapa daba.

33. SIX DAYS

God creating
The milliard universes,
Besides this third
Blue-green planet,
Pan-isolating six seconds.
Your dilemma?
Had a problem
Explaining minutes,
Seconds, milliseconds,
Elementary trigonometry,
To cocoon minds
Like yours.
He made it simple.

34. MINIMUM EFFORT

If you can,
Strike flint into gushing streams,
Un-flu common flu,
Command myriad frogs
March to the palace,
Bed with bed-bugs,
Touch the blind to see, even vaguely,
Say your sins are forgiven,
Breathe in, breathe out,
Count one to thirteen
In your grave clothes.
He furnished a desert table,
Opened the windows of Heaven;
Rained angel's corn bread,
Blew in feathered fowls.
Proclaim your dollared destiny,
Invent flies, if you can,
Speke the universe swirling,
Free, out of opaque vacuum.

35. **AMETHYST PURPLE**

Would you pace, peck these dusty trails of Galilee,
Truly Lamb of God born, Messiah anointed sent?
I wallow in this prison mire, God truly mighty,
Unloose my camel belt for a kiss sin I did not kiss?
Did I eat honey sautéed locust for a jailer's prize,
Shouted back to the wilderness mountain echoes,
"Fire to the Roman imperialists!" for toddler's game?

Children of royals are dressed in amethyst purple;
Still you peddle and peck these dusty roads of Galilee,
Dressed in earth colours: Yellow ochre, late rite brown.
Honored carriages are escorted by galloping fanfare.
Hark! Your followers, men of fish smell, enticing nonentity.

A face uncomely, innocent, plain, nondescript,
Acquainted with grief; the grief of sucking widows,
Unattractive, without political poise, military metal.
Awaited a Zealot's recital, a rhyme, a liberator's goalmouth.
In childlike parables and ancient proverbs, you supplicated
Of Kingdom come, of peace, love, and joy, hollow gong,
Oblivious of palisade Roman presence on the ground.

Confederate human fanfare with Roman Palisade march.
Fish smell I will celebrate, bridal royals I will anoint.
Did you go to the Jordan to see reeds waving in the wind?
To the desert wilderness to witness palace glint, royals,
Dressed in amethyst purple, in zestful breast plates?

Except the curtains of your eyes be drawn, you stumble still,
While I peddle and peck these dusty roads of Galilee.

OF CHURCH

His Church
Unlike ours

36. THE USUAL SANDWICH

Hymn, prayer, hymn,
Announcements,
15 minutes sermon,
Benediction,
Hymn.

37. COMFORTABLE PEOPLE

Comfortable people,
Born, padded, into nestles,
Like pigeonlets, groomed,
Like Butterfly Gladioli's
In full bloom,
Inherit the middle-class cream cake,
Even at the age of eighteen.

Comfortable people
Thank God, now the gods,
For not breeding them
On the sub-Saharan death-beds,
Where men dig the dying sands,
Only to circle in vicious Hades
Year after year.

Have forgotten to say Grace
Before any meal,
Simply in the name of Hamburger and Coke,
And the Chinese takeout,

That comes easy on the phone.
That, they say too,
Is not evil,
Since jogging once a week
Takes care of the extra fat.

Comfortable people
On ergonomically perfect assembly lines
Will make their blood cells run, chase,
The zero stress punch machines
That now think with you on the screen.
Will die; even die,
For the acoustically
Under two decibels,
Gravity-free chamber bliss:
A concept of work,
And a hard-won reward,
For years of sweat drops at school.

Comfortable people
Holiday dream of Cleopatra-baths,
With water heated to body temperature,
Wondering how one recreates
Youthful days with girls at school.

Comfortable people are happy
To keep to their middle-class pews,
Let the professionals do their thing,
Love to hear dog-collared men
Pile their Sunday buffet plates
With Greek and Hebrew words,
Which makes everyone feel so clever.
But then comfortable people are happy
When the benediction is at long last pronounced,
And have to head for the Sunday roast,

Which was long switched off
In the microwave.

Comfortable people
Home and dry in church cloisters,
Elders board meetings, drinking tea
And Bourbon biscuits,
And ladies in their peaceful hats,
Sharing herbal lip-ace tints,
And "baby and mother" aces tints,
Have forgotten the mother of all aces:
"Go into the whole world ..."
... Into the whole world ...
And the triple ace:
Multiply, subdue, fill the earth.

I saw a comfortable one
Giggling at a drunk, wounded wino.
Have forgotten, if not by grace,
They too would have surfaced
A wined, wounded drunk.
Have forgotten this old earth
Is sliding toward hell,
As fast as hell toward earth.
And he said, "Yes, that's true,
But I am home and dry
In this cloister, having tea
And Bourbon biscuits."

38. LOUD AS PENTECOST

They say
I am a crazy charismatic,
A bubbling locomotive,
A junk rail wagon rolling,
Full of cheap exhaust theology.

They say
I am a frustrated religious cockroach,
A social bug that thinks
Bigger than his purse.

They call it
Chronic rat-race complex.
I call it faith.
I sure can differentiate between
Faith and fantasy;
My ecstasy is in-house, genuine.

My rap is automatic,
But my nap phlegmatic,
My tambourine banging,
Resurgent-loud.
When the Spirit is moving,
I roll like the Rolling Stones,
Drugged not with the Hebrides gin,
But with the original din,
For my neck up is clear.

When I pray for the sick,
It's time for the medics to glove off.
My aisle tumble is upper-roomed,
Only a craze for my lover.
I show it, breathe it, cantillate it.

My lover deserves some noise,
As loud as Pentecost,
Apostle Peter chairing.
If you think my love-sound is deafening
And prefer it as dead as walnut pews,
Then wait till you hit heaven.

39. **THE DIVINE AIRWAYS FLIGHT**

Show some excitement,
A rhapsodic elation,
Especially
If you know that you know that you know.
Make the fete, a holy revel,
Especially
If you know that you won, without winning,
For that is grace defined.
Bubble it, and why not?
The holy fathers did it and weren't ashamed.
Lie down prostrate if you must lie down,
Makes sense when the feeling is deep inside.

Kneel your prayers, your polyester knees,
That's why they invented the dry cleaning business.
Bang those tambourines; bang them,
You can't out do Miriam's band, can you?
Show some excitement.
There is no confusion, is there?
We know what is wild, but dead,
And what is wild and legitimate.

Why the apology, why the apathy?
You have been declared free,
Canonized a saint for basically doing nothing.
Why the guilt?
What have you stolen?

You have grabbed nothing
Except the keys of the kingdom;
It was yours from the beginning, anyway.

Show up;
You are part of the road engineers,
Preparing the way of the Lord.
Show up;
It is servanthood and brotherhood in the hood.
It is first things first.
Show up;
You are part of the surgery team,
Every dry bone, bone to bone, becoming flesh.
You have got a job to do, it's a command:
Preach the Gospel to every creature,
Even to trees; Billy Graham did it.
Show up;
Be counted among the brave.
We've got the power
To dethrone kings and set up governments.
Raise the banners high,
Flutter its victory colours,
Give the devil a run for his folly,
It is him who is going out for eternity
With his tail between his legs.
Blow the Vuvuzella trumpet loud;
The Lord is risen,
Leaving Buddha and Mohamed behind.

Dance!
Don't say "I am Caucasian."
I say, Dance!
Don't say, "I am not that low."
King David wasn't low, was he?
Dance till you drop dead;

Possibly the best way of dying.

Clap your hands,
Because the Bible says so.
Clap your hands!
They won't get blistered;
Only your stupid pride will.

Raise those holy hands to the Lord!
Maybe you shouldn't,
If they aren't holy.
Raise those hands to the Lord.
No hand is denominational;
They were created
To veto out dead creed.

Expect a miracle every day;
Expect a miracle.
Audacity presupposes it archaic, antediluvian,
But let me ask you this:
Two billion up tired and wretched,
Or two billion up fired, sorrow-free,
Which is better?
To walk out healed, clean and free,
Or to walk out healed, flat broke, insolvent,
Which is better?

Don't say, "Make it short, preacher."
Never heard anyone say to a flat screen,
"Make it short and sweet, creature."
But you sit at that perpetual tube, LCD, DSQ,
Whatever the Japanese will call it next,
Hours on end, popcorn and all,
Watching woman marries uncle,
And uncle marries daughter,

Daughter shoots uncle,
And daughter marries woman,
And you call that clever, glib.

Shout it,
And make it loud.
"Why shout?" you ask. "God is not deaf."
I say, "Why shout?
The football skin isn't deaf either."
So shout it;
We are the ones in control,
Not the USA.
A few night shouts
Could mint you some USD.
Remember, a few night shouts,
A few fasts and prostrate falls
Brought down the Berlin Wall.

Sing it,
In whichever key and tongue.
We have a future and a hope;
It us who will sing the song of the beloved
When our divine airways flight
Touches down on that golden runway.

40. FOUNDATIONS

In the past we prayed with hands folded in;
Now we pray with hands lifted out to God.
In the past we rejoiced over our democracy and independence;
Now we are glad to be subject to one another.
Our meetings lasted exactly one hour, timed by the sand clock;
Now they last as long as they have to last.
In the past the Pastor was an employee of the Board of Deacons;
Now the Elders and Deacons are disciples of the Pastor.
We preached that baptism wasn't necessary to salvation;

Now we know that salvation comes by faith and baptism.
We preached salvation of the soul, and the soul-trains; fast to heaven;
Now we say, yes, but not yet. He said, "Send the soul-trains to the nations."
We spoke against speaking in tongues;
Now we wonder how we ever existed without speaking in tongues.
In the past we entered the temples on tiptoe because God was there;
We enter now with dancing and leaping because God is there.

We changed those foundations; exchanged his spirit for papal prints;
Became Baptists, Methodists, Presbyterians, and many such spires,
Began to fear confronting men with repentance and baptism,
And turned to innocent babblings whose only complex
Was cold water smeared cross their Anglican faces.
We became suspicious of praying to someone unlike our kin,
So we catholicized in Mother Mary, just in case.
That Gospel seemed too simple to be true,
So we called in theologians and they made it a social science.
Now we can't even distinguish between theology of liberation
And liberation of theology.
We started well as Pentecostals, snooped by chilling inner feel,
But slowly our hallelujah hand clapping
Faded away behind ecclesiastical protocol.

But thank God we are now being brought back to those foundations.
Thank God His Spirit is here; his Glory is come.
He is leading us now to see that:
Once we were not a people, haters of God, accursed,
But now we are the beloved of God, a blessed nation;
Now we are the building of God, the cedar of Lebanon.
We were sustained only by the lulling of our piped organs;
Now we are a prophetic lot, an army of God,
A theocracy with one glorious King, our greatest pride.
We were once strangers, aliens, cast a camp;
Now we are his friends, gathered to be the inhabitants of Zion,
The city of God, a new race, a new generation,

Fit for his dwelling place, the New Jerusalem.

41. DENOMINATIONAL SHROUD

I am not a Pentecostal, though I throb and bubble quite a bit;
I swear the Lord hears me clear when I use his own tongue.
I am not a Charismatic, although my car is automatic.
I don't have to engage gears if some brain has already automated it for me.
I am neither a holy roller nor a sinful roller; I only do what pleases the Father.
I am neither a Southern Baptist nor Northern Baptist; that's for the Americans
    to decide.
I was baptized in an Edinburgh font, in heated water, so watch out!
I am not a Presbyterian, though I believe in the presbytery and in the
    Best Three.
In fact, I am an elder in my church, if that means anything to you.
I am not a Methodist, but the way I snore during a boring sermon is
    quite meticulous.
I am not sure whether I am a Seventh Day Adventist or a Sixth Day Adventist;
I won't care much whether Sunday was held on Sunday or on Wednesday.
I am definitely an Anglican, because that is where I was born, but believe
    you me,
I will not die where I was born; a man must move on, you know.
I am part of the catholic global, but that does not make me Roman Catholic.
If Jesus has already done it all, then why do we need two or three
    Holy Rosaries?
I do understand, though, why the Roman Catholics are astounded by the
    virgin birth;
It's quite a brief to find a girl, who is truly virgin intact, with the wedding
    cake uncut.
If you find one, especially these days of easy champagne toasting, marry
    her, fast.
I admire anyone who cracks ecclesiastical fallacy, so for that matter I
    am Lutheran.
I admire anyone who says, "Back to the Bible; keep it simple, stupid—KISS.
Kiss the Son, not the Sun; the difference is the distance between you and
    the Bible.

In all, be it nonsensical, theological witticism, but befuddling, it's for you
    to decide.
This one is one, this one is sure: the Spirit of Truth, when he comes,
He will lead us to all truth, including political and economic truth.
He will weave you through all denominational shrouds,
Incising between myth and fact, sense and nonsense, half-truth and true truth.

42. HEAVENLY CRAFT

They say that
Speaking in tongues
Is for the emotionally ill,
That miracles were for the days
Of Cornelius and folk like that.
Rather be a Baptist
And be counted among
The right-thinking members of society.

They say this trend
Toward hand clapping
And Tambourine banging
Is taking Heaven's Boards of Directors
For a ride.
Want it straight and clean
From the Annual General Meeting.

They ask
How can one fast once a week,
With executive lunches booked on the net,
And the wife, epicurean wiz cook.
They say pursing out one-in-ten
Is only possible when the parking lights,
On Wall Street are all turned green.
But as long as the Limited Resource Law applies,
We all must expect a swift karate chop
Below our economic belts.

They say
Going to the Wednesday prayer meet
Can't be possible with the professionals heavy on the telly,
And Hollywood babes glazing their lips even redder,
And work brought home from office,
As if you were sitting an MBA exam.

This door-to-door soul marking
Is embarrassing to our professional tints,
And our neighbourhood image feel.
How does a tint mate drop by and find you
Calling on some Heavenly godfather?

"Respect your three thousand cc Japanese metal," they say.
"Drive like you are part of the Hood."
Then I answered, "All these I do for my lover,
And for my three billion cc Heavenly craft
That glides at the speed of thought,
And for my sure mansion whose reception hall alone
Makes the White House level a beach-sand child play."

43. TWO SIPS OF WINE

To be radical
Is to sit your blue jean buttons on the mirror-planed pews,
Gaze beyond the point where the Calvary wood crosses,
And say, "Abba Father," without a comma, without blinking.
Is to take two sips of the communion wine,
While the fair robed priest counts one to fifteen,
Lest you summarize his goblet in a single swipe.

To be radical
Is to fan divine flame beneath all ecclesiastical mysticism,
Shun all impious liturgies, cloistered religious compunction,
Allow the Holy Spirit rewrite the order of service
On heart shaped papers, devoid of discotheque muddle

And superfluous middle-class morality,
Synthesize vibes that exact life-transformation solo.

It is cultured to pace European church architecture; it is art.
Wondered though how I dedicate architectonic fallacy, heathen knick-knacks,
Give them spiritual dictum, only to please the owners of stones:
Spires that point sky-ward to nonentity, never to celebrate celestial graces,
Pulpits, Baptismal fonts, high minded naves, sequesters subterfuge,
Holy tables, mere colonial extortion of African mahogany,
Stained glasses tinged fair gospel, tarnished authentic spirituality,
Flying buttresses that prop nothing but agnostic capitalism,
Vestries that conceal the secret sin-games of reverent fathers,
Confession booths that shield the maladies of fallen humanity.

To be radical
Is to diffuse the laws of stability and symmetry,
For the search of dynamism and eccentricity,
To question justified and supported stupidity
For unpopular and searching madness,
Like querying the downward fall of apples,
And love for any work of Picasso.

Once I asked my pastor
How the sermon on the starving Somalis
Plumuled out of his bookshelf, naked, without a heart cover.
I dared him brave a debate with fanatical whiskery Marxist,
Called for a spat with a spiritless atheist, expand his mind.
I invited the entire board of deacons out, dress code casual,
For a bowling game at the mall, drink malt, and asked,
"Did Jesus ever laugh, and who paid the insurance cover
On the thousand swine that drowned down the cliff?"

To be radical
Is to halt this compass-less Bible study
On the book of Ezra, endless lessons from September Eleven,

Freeze all the ball games, biscuit-teas at the church hall,
And ask the mother of all questions,
"We are busy cutting a road through the forest,
But are we in the right forest in the first place?
And where, for Christ's sake, is that road leading?"

To be radical
Is to risk a spot in the march toward the City Hall
And shout, "Down with the Tsars; down with corruption!"
And to wipe your eyes with the holy communion napkin,
Not only because of the tears in your heart,
But because of the teargas in your eyes.
Is to write in the papers, "Enough is enough of this rot,"
And to insist the rot is taken off the rubbish bins.

If church was not meant to be a social hub
For right-wing, middle-class apple pies,
Then what are we doing here, in our Sunday best,
And ladies in their over-sexed slit skirts,
And the helpless pastors at the door saying,
"Thank you, come again"?

OF FAITH

My faith is built on nothing less ...

44. FAITHLESS WORMS

they say
this old earth
will roll, will stagger
and cough under its own
creative genius,
and fear, they say,
we will populate
this blue-green ball
till we can only grow
inward into our tummies.

that
our only hope
is to breed
the miracle ringworm;
the new high protein snack,
as tasty
as your chocolate thought,
and a super culture
that can even breathe argon gas
on planet mars.

they say
Christ is coming back,
bursting through the skies;
a rescue operation,
his beloved,
petrified,

shredded-cabbaged,
daunted by the antichrist.
i say, "no.
a victory celebration,
a pointed
two-edged sword,
at the down-damned antichrist,
and the father of all lies,
brought salvation to the nations."

they say
this world will end
in some third world war
nuclear holocaust,
with the Russians killing
the Americans seven times over,
Americans killing Russians thirteen times over,
and every dead person killed
twenty-five times over.

well,
if that lives with you,
then bunker two more metres,
reinforce your concrete cover quick.
but as for me,
he has gone to prepare
a new earth;
emancipated nations,
like new heaven,
where peace, joy,
loves us all.

45. DIVINE-CASUAL

Every time I hear a tourist craft
Jet off to Neptune or such like colonies,
Their full throttle take off sound
Levels a blast from the London Philharmonic Orchestra
Playing, "Hark! My Redeemer," in F-sharp minor.
Proudly 187 roomed, postmodern architectonic studio
Next to the spaceship landing pad, Floor 2,937,
New Jerusalem condominium, mixed development,
Is my new abode, to be specific.

Entire cube has no need of air-con, podium lights,
Cause He is the SON and the SUN.

Trisember thirteenth, all lifts stop at floor 2,937,
For that will be my 6,000th birth day.
Dress code: divine-casual. Trust you'll come,
Cause the Lord Himself will be there,
So is the gal who used to be my wife,
And Sam. You remember Sam, my son then?
He now plays Oboe at the Morning Star Festival.

46. ONCE AN AMOEBA

How can the devil tell me that my ancestors were baboons?
That the universe was a product of chance,
An outcome of some cosmic chaos;
That life on this planet was the consequence
Of some electro-chemical disturbances,
Resulting in the "runaway" internally generated nuclear fission,
Producing amino acids that found it fit
To organize themselves into living cells?

How can the devil tell me
That I was once some kind of amoeba,

A blob of protoplasm
Floating on that lethal primeval sea?
That the amoeba, by natural selection,
Generated into some kind of creature
That resembles a cross
Between the great Australian lizard
And a roll of barbed wire!
And that this bionic being generated and again generated
Into an ape-like creature,
Which is supposed to be my ancestor?

Well, if you want to be the nephew
Of some old celebrating baboon,
That's your own problem.
But as for me,
I am the son of the MOST HIGH GOD,
Created in his own image,
With all systems set.

47. ARMAGEDDON BLOOD

Kremlin Square bathes red in Armageddon blood;
The Statue of Liberty, its ice cream cone
Firmly held, crumbles to a miserable heap.
The Union Jack flies permanently at half-mast;
Deeply lamenting the children of the isles:
"Cross the channel quickly, for Britannia is dead forever."
Then will I fix my gaze to the Hill of the Skull,
Confident its wood, whets strong still.

The horns we adore much turn into brute-dictators,
Bars of gold; the bars once saluted with a long-live smile
Corrode with acid rain that broods human translucency,
When Gibraltar finds it safer to hide under the sea,
Industrial gears grind down and halt, smell of burnt oil welcome,
Familiar Equator drum sounds fade with convecting winds.

Swathing peace pierced sharply in the West, in the waist.
Fair faced cassone vaults declared insolvent, zeros simplified,
Bitter sorghum bread, signed with joy, the object of all queues.
Friends and fiends alike scurrilously spit, "Spit on his face, his toil."
See Moslems, Hindus, Christians capsule now in exact matrimony."
But will gin down my throat soothe trepidation, future form,
A sure signal of His grand finale, my sure end, my sufficiency?

Remnants reject history settled outside His story, all ages concluded,
Would rather starve to death than print credit cards on their skins,
Sign off their birth rights for dehydrated barley loaves, join the queue.
New York lies on her death bed; The Jerusalem baby is born.
My ash bed behind I wield the Old Book at the king of lies,
"I am not yet history in this place; I perceived this plot before,
A doomsday, pessimist's alarm, an escapist cave to some a fairy tale.
Watch now the Master's sleeves, history book of Heaven lived."

48. NEXT TIME

Next time you plan to dream,
Dream of baby-blue skies
With peace sparrows
Patrolling God's Heaven.

Next time you plan to dream,
Dream of you
Bathing in rainbow shadows,
Leaping on lime-green meadows.
Watch those peace sparrows again;
They think it is us
Who are on the wrong side of Heaven.

Next time you have time
To look at the lily carpets,
See their duty is to clothe the river valleys,
And they are not even paid a salary,

But they are happy just to be there,
Like rose buds
That distil your sweet herbal gins for free.
Next time you are in church,
Paying your dues,
See it as paying your rent
For living here on planet earth.

Next time you open your mouth
To sing a hymn to God,
Remember the larks;
They do it all the time,
Giving it all they got,
Yet they plane no pews to sit on.

Next time you kneel down to pray,
Thank the good Lord
For creating the baby-blue skies.
Let your thanks giving
Not only be
Now, for making your fingertips
Print the Japanese yen, the green paper-dream,
But thank God for creating God,
For only God can do that.

Next time you give time to your kids,
Remember, sooner it will be too late
For them to giggle on your laps.
Any truth you truth with them
Goes down in history
As gems buried down in future
Just for them.

Next time you are in the bathroom,
As naked as Eden,

Remember that at that very moment,
You are at your best,
Like Adam and Eve
Before they leafed on their sin.
So next time you have a problem in your soul,
Go to the bathroom, turn on the shower,
And sing those lark-hymns to God again.

Next time you knee your marriage,
Especially in these days
When prayer is a trifle act,
When the world is saying
Marriage is only for people
Who haven't yet discovered
The pleasant secret freedom
Of living like wild goats,
Remember that God split up man's atom
To make him real man.

49. EVIDENCE

Evidence was a seminal youth musical that changed the lives of many young Christian people in 1970s Nairobi. The musical theme was centred on the return of Christ. Many church leaders around Nairobi were concerned and skeptical about the legitimacy of the gathering/fellowship at Nairobi University, Ufungamano house of the youths, as a direct result of this musical.

A five Richter scale quake sounded it,
The Nations newspaper reported it,
The who is who clergies in Nairobi robes
Urgently conferred, "Who are these Evidence youth,
Rocking the city with their white flame doctrine?
Our kids used to evacuate before the benediction pronounced;
Now we evacuate before they complete their first session.
And who are the leaders of this raw rock band?
Could it be they are performing what we have failed?

If we pounce them down-hard, won't we be fighting against God?
This look like a live-sized revival, but it's a band of raw rock.

And the white flame spread wide with its fire-tongue;
Indians got it; Moslems got saved and addicted.
Malignant cells evaporated, cavities filled instantly,
Youth visions lived live, and dreams reported next.
Entire schools altered, turned U turns, no questions asked.
Silver's starter engine, a question most spires missed:
"If Christ was coming back that soon, could be today,
Could be tomorrow, bursting through the clouds,
What kind of life then should we live?
Or you prefer to hang around when the antichrist hangs around?"
This dry ice, hard prayed, converted into choreographed musical
Was all He needed to know that someone was serious.
Little did Silver know that the Spirit was to burst men's hearts,
Was sweet to ear, was hard to fear, seeing cavities filled.
Douglas insisted, "After your U turn, you get baptized in fire, now;
You leave your sex friends; now, you live His right now.
And you see God's power in your life, in your family, work, now."
And for sure more malignant cells evaporated, cavities filled instantly,
Entire families got saved; nuns came, bowed down their sins.
Elders boards agreed, "This surely is a lived-sized revival."
Evidence of His soon return.
You came to the Ufungamano meeting thirty minutes early;
You were late, had to sit outside, peep from the windows.
Even peeping through the windows got your God-shaped cavities filled.

School doors, church doors, families opened to the mustard seed.
And the mustard-kid tree grew and grew, filling the globe:
Fowls lodging in Kenya, Nigeria, Malawi with Harriet Muruiki;
Didn't spare India with Gachiko there thickly;
Australia with Steve Odonga, missionary Lucy Lutara in the UK,
Shannon Tito, Don, gospel singer, Vancouver, Canada,
Steve and Beatrice Langa, Youth leaders, expotentiary,

Worship pillars Jack and Joyce Odongo, anything worship.
Now Pastor Alan Kisaka, California, USA
Now Pastor Kwame Rubadiri, Washington, USA
David Seda with MicroSoft or NASA, who knows
Moisari, Charles, Mutua, Matu, Paul, Betty, now in Heaven, we know.

Could go on. Downstream ripples, splinter sets exploded:
All calling themselves "Miros," black, saved, and proud.

Dentist, International Leadership pundits James and Lorna Magara;
Damoni Kitabire, World Bank, World trotter; Hellen Lutara, Hospital owner;
No-nonsense government stones, Allen Kagina, Jeniffer Musisi;
World Vision desk, Edward Mubirn, Washington, D.C, USA;
Lawyers, police chiefs, pastors, restaurant owners, mega farmers like
    Chris Lutara,
Kingfishers everywhere and all who understood the word Miro and the
    Miro bond.

Pastor Marvin Thomas did clear his throat, at the Who's Who clergies,
"These Evidence youths are performing what we have failed;
Leave them alone, we all stand to gain from their wit."

50. INTERLUDE GIFT

In heaven, where pink clouds sing to each other,
There are no marriages, baby cots, pampers,
Giggling kids in Sunday school, challenging future brains,
Asking why two plus two makes four and not three.
When the green bottle is popped, silly strings fill the air,
And the wedding dance is asked for; dance your love-heart out.
You remain pinned to the wall, save for a love-hate pander.
Will the couple barter rings for strangers' smiles, for gall goblet?
Revisit the altar, revisit the priest's vestry, exchange tears,
Coerce a smile, romance your love-shaped heart again.

Appreciate every ticking minute of this interlude gift,
Of life on this planet earth, one earth, on this solar soup.
Whistle that menial job, the old Boy Scouts' way;
Flip the pancake in the air as you do the Whola-Whola.
Do all you can, can all you do, leave the rest to God.

Enjoy the humble side the town you're in.
Remember others would drown a raft just to land your shores.
Be proud of the colour of your animal skin. Someone had to be black,
Someone had to be white, creating two edges for all colours in between.
Remember the story of the white missionary kid living in the Congo.
He said, "Dad, when I grow up, I'd like to be an African."
His mango tree playing mates were all black, and that's what mattered.
Greet every stranger you meet along the way with a smile;
It proves you are a child of the universe, within the same colour rainbow.
Greet every flower, whether red or blue, with a "bend down, sample my scent."
It proves you love all God's creation, not just Italian cars and shredded jeans.

Don't eye your neighbour's car too much; in the final count,
They are all unregenerate mobile metals, destined for the bin.
Marvel not that mobile phone that even recognizes one's body scent.
Remember, in only six months' time, it will be obsolete, debunked junk.

Be proud that God created you, you; if the Gurus were right,
In this life you would be a moth, but God created you, you,
With all systems going, all loyal to the central nervous code.
So next time you are in front of a mirror, shout "Hallelujah,"
That the Gurus are no more right, no more exacting
Than Hottentots thinking that an aeroplane is
A slowed down shooting star, a polar bird to its sabbatical.

Were I you, I would check, recheck, these image builders,
Motivational pundits transporting us all beyond His sublime line.
You are already body-built in God's own image,
Every skin cell divinely down-loaded, every hair GPS placed

Precisely. He knows your coming in and your going out,
Sees your thoughts wandering, naked, between nonentity and nonentity,
Your prayers lurking behind tear drops and evaporating smiles,
And tired face, tired body, being beaten to resemble His Son to come.

51. LAZY NEWTON GLOW-WORM PEAKS

Seated here together, still, on the same inert bench,
Pendulum to your intimidating door gesture.
Am I some kind of obtuse, sun bathed newt,
Confused warthog, an indolent monitor lizard,
Humble bellboy, peddling unwheeled luggage?
Reverence, veneration applied, toil acknowledged?
One day I will prove, sway you, believe,
I'm no languid bone, easy summer paw-paw,
The humble bellboy peddling unwheeled luggage.

God's masks are the mirrors we reflect in,
But even newts, mauve colours or not,
Like goggle-eyed, extra-terrestrial elves,
Weren't met morphed from the beginning.
His marks are the reverent temperaments,
Maybe melancholic, maybe choleric.
Try His divine ex-rays, crystal vantage point;
You'll find I'm neither stupid nor lazy.

Always dreamt myself prearranged, seated,
On glow-worm peaks, smiling at my inside-out,
At my divine destiny attained, acclimatized,
Colours that are true, my polished vestibules.

Sinful thoughts, sinful though, through and through,
Are my insides, but He is still at it, chipping,
Clipping out aggravated edges, perfecting colours.
This futile task, you say, of making me sit
On glow-worm peaks, is it not futile, pitiful?

Multiple maladies, I have confessed, forsaken,
No longer watch sensual soap operas, anything triple-x.
Armoured gear I have cloaked, accessories and all,
Forsaken all attempts to coercible mirror-reflections
Of a stranger's, friend's, foe's image of me.
One day you'll know, not swayed, persuaded,
He was neither lazy nor stupid, ignored, uninterested,
Perfecting the colours of my vestibules.

52. FALLEN SKIN.

*About thirty years ago, I used to get very cross with one of my nephews regarding
his drinking and laziness in his studies. One day I gave him beating on his bare
buttocks, as is our culture in disciplining such a person. However, my mother told
me to be soft on his buttocks, for we are all fallen creatures requiring forgiveness
and kindness from God.*

Leave him alone;
Be soft on his back;
He's an only a child;
Unless you want him
To skip a generation
Like Michael Jackson.

Mother would say,
Leave them alone.
What do you expect
Of their brutish ways?
Marriage without the cross
Is like a T-Junction
Without a billboard.

Be soft on her stony heart;
Remember the Lord
Was hard on Pharisees, hypocrites,
But not sinners like you and me.

What do you expect of her?
She is not born again,
Touched by the fire-tongue;
At least she plays no hide and seek with pews.

Mother would say,
Leave him alone,
What do you expect of his lips?
They are no different from his back.
They are both a fallen skin.
Unless scorched by divine embers,
They'll go the same way of man;
Little demon's yo-yo game.

Don't laugh at her breasts;
They are the only ones she got.
If she had money like Michael Jackson,
She would help God with plastic surgery,
Make boobs as large as a jack tree fruit.
She tried to paint her skin apricot yellow,
But look at what she got;
A hue between Desert Pink
And French Ultra-marine!

Without a revelation,
He read all volumes
In the religious cellar-secrets.
But look where he wound up:
A fooled-face, debunked Mongolian monk.
Without Grace.
He tried to appease God,
Became a volunteer corp in India,
Retrieving corpses on the Ganges.
See what he got in eternity raw now:
A volunteer corpse on the river of life.

Without salvation,
He is like you and me
Before mercy sought us out:
Wanting, down to our pants.
So, at best, intercede for him.
Some drag out, forced by fire;
Others, with a mother's care.
Mother them the way of life.

You cried,
And indeed, I cried too,
That he died like a bog-dog.
But without the cross,
Going to eternity without Christ
Is like going to a livid, insane dentist
With his syringes on the ready.

53. MULISH DOORS

Midnight candles, wearied drawing boards, waking with the birds;
Rewarded with air-burgers, bread of sorrows, and cocktail promises.
Pundit's seminars attended, self-battering drills, prosperity manuals read,
Settled for aborted dreams, futile drips from deactivated springs, vacuum paid.
Yet I pay my tithes, recite my prayers the way my mother taught me,
Have shunned all meats, red or white, but the kilos locate where they locate.
Tried jogging with the morning mist; you'll agree I am no indolent lizard.
My lot a delayed gratification, a pointing signboard, or a relentless doom?
Far behind schedule, my destiny discharge gazes in an empty horizon,
Stuck with my prophetic vistas; holding firm to history written in heaven.
Non-comparable peers enjoy quietude, peace, satisfied in goblet sundowners,
And laze with peacocks on their Sunday afternoon bowling greens.
Vital now is divine speed, like Prophet Elijah's foot race, pass chariots,
Divine favour than reward-less toil, son of promise than an Ishmael birth.

His word tutors, reveals the prince of the air is alert at his work,
With sons, agents, aldermen conscripted only to giggle at my loss.
Targeting A-plus students, God's super anointed like you and me.
Has kept the gates, lock and key, interfered with heaven's conduits;
Has ruptured my bank accounts, laid me flat in excruciating ash trays.
His ageless mandate, schema simple, his fugitive, heinous smile, clear:
To disarm, disfigure, disorganize, discomfort, dismiss, disarray, distort,
And all the diseased dices he dishes to his disdained, decimated dregs.
Now I know where the eternal puzzle lay, the ageless secret, the plot;
I know the keys to unlock, unchain, kick open, command open
Those ancient gates, those obstinate, mulish, obdurate doors;
Give a bulldog bark at his disdained dregs too, wave a fiery sword
At his futile task to reduce me to cold clinker, share molten eternity with him.
The power to amputate his hind limbs near my lip; it's that close.
Have the keys to unlock his secret vaults, peep into his wicked spell notes.

54. MILLISECONDS AWAY

When the killer led
Darts through my inner gray,
The squeaking sound of the wheel
Folds me severed, severely,
Into a sudden halt.
Rushed I am then
To my dutied friends;
White and all in white,
Who must recite
The Hypocrite's Oath quick.
They stretch,
Cut and uncut;
They do like dutied friends.
But as sure
As the sun must rise,
Morning by morning
From its sleeping bed,
Slowly with agony,

They unglove,
Remove those tubes,
Syringes, gloves, masks,
And turn all knobs
To Position "Off."

No one speaks
Except tears
Calling on each other,
"Look, look,
He is leaving us,
Leaving.
No, may it never be."
The tears drop.

But as sure
As the sun must rise,
Morning by morning
From its sleeping bed,
Life must come
To one end,
And at the end, life
Must gate the way
To LIFE.

Then immediately,
As soon as immediate,
Will I open my eyes
To the spirit world,
To a flaming chariot
And a winged friend
In a waiting smile.
Then I will know
That the streets
Of pure gold,

Of purer gold,
Are only milliseconds away.

And those
Of our numbers gone before,
Will welcome greet me,
"Well done, friend.
Why did you take so long?
Come on in."

55. WORM EYE VIEW

This great green-blue ball,
Propped
To our galaxy   -   is astronomy.

The Empire State stones,
Viewed with a sea-horse gaze   -   is infinity.

God creating God   -   is divinity.

Three score and ten
Years promised,
Plucked   -   I pondered; is eschatology.
From squillion
Years of eternity's plan

Winning without winning   -   is Grace.

Years of toil,
Years of pain
On this cruel grit,
Poached   -   our prime life
From His grand-finale   mirrored
          to His great love.

56. **FAITH IS**

Posted in the future, delivered now,
The substance of your stuff, clear.
Raise your glass, click the crystals,
Join in the duplicity cocktail talk.
Any circle, any clique, any confab,
Whether on parametric economic recovery curve,
Few apprehend, rest invent, cleverly.
Robe in the manner of the hood,
And the hood robe you appertain.
Confess it, confirm its coming, blink not,
Work it, work towards it, it will live.

Flag the evidence, your belief gear,
Real, may be easy, maybe not;
A work your fingers can dip,
Any work your fingertips can tip,
Hebrews eleven views it taught.
Abraham displayed a raised knife,
The blood-issue woman
Her concern, "If only, if only,"
Touched His garment's hem,
Was evidence enough.

57. **INSIDE STORY**

You masked your face
With bars of silver,
Duped cleverly, our band,
Counting Thomas duped
At the last table,
Not my brain-child.
A crooked branch from the start,
Bent to notoriety, before His gain.
Though those pieces glitter,

Would they net mirrored robes?
See, Rome is here, still,
But your inner gutter
Has gushed you
Straight into hell.

OF SON-LIKE PEOPLE

"I want to know Christ—yes, to know the power of his resurrection and participation in his suffering, becoming like him in his death" (Philippians 3:10, NIV). In the Bible, Jesus speaks to the people of His time about humility. He said that whoever is least and humbles himself will be exalted, and the one who is exalted will be humbled (Matthew 23:12). Jesus was speaking to the religious folks of His time, saying that all of the things they did to make themselves look important were not authentic or God honouring. Being Son-like means having the heart of Christ. O'City writes about family and friends who he believes demonstrated this authentic leadership like Christ.

> *That have influenced me the most,*
> *Aren't exactly eccentrics.*
> *They aren't like you and me either.*

82. CHARLES OWOR:
(TELL YOUR BROTHER)

Tell your brother to leave politics alone.
He may be a clever lawyer;
He should know better.
The world is ruled only by grade C students.
A classroom chalk may boast the same girth
As an eleven-millimetre calibre brass-plated shot,
But do they perform the same errands?

Tell your brother to leave politics alone.
Politics is a dirty game, they say,
Like visiting your favourite floozy;
It is fun, but no one tells you
The devil giggles with every condom slipped.
It's not about who you are not hurting,
But who you don't think you are hurting.

Leave politics to us.
He may be a good orator, best television debater,
But he doesn't have the needed social lubricant.
These days it's the purse that pushes, purges,
It's which bodyguard, godfather you have in money places.
For me, I have neither, so I wait, only to cast my vote
To whoever can un-canyon potholes on my side of town.
Moreover, what future is there that we are all clamouring for?
Even America, the great, can no longer crystal ball ten years at a time.
What matters is food on the tables, children at school,
Completing that house before the guards change.
Are we not all preparing for that one world government,
Ruled by some Italian Pasta living in Brussels or wherever?
You see, politics is no longer about representation and repression,
But about swift image reflection and shrewd doppelganger,
Not taught in law schools, but in pubs and gin places.
Politics is no more about democracy and consensus set,
Dictators won't retire otherwise in some EU-frill outfit.
It's about staying afloat and once afloat, how much to tuck away, safe.
Tell your brother to stop talking intellectual bullshit:
Egalitarianism, effusive alms, effervescent economy and effective efface.
These are words that are fit only for the university senior staffrooms.
Those of us who sit always in the VIP daises know better.
We know where to peg when the champagne bottle is being popped,
And a fair guess which row the serving cake will run out.

Equity yes, but, we are talking about the laws of limited supply,
Especially in this black granite part of the world.
Listen, your brother is still young, has a young wife, young children,
Why can't he be like the other Christians:
Peace loving, law abiding, naively stupid, and toothless?
And we like it that way:
Making noise only when the curtain is down, the drama ended,
And strut in at the scene when the butchering is over,
Good at not telling lies, poor at not telling the truth,

Seeing humanity go to rot, forgetting once were resident in death mire.
For that I admire Charles' enthusiasm and humanitarian concern.

Tell your brother
Politics is not about conscience or no conscience,
That is for the clergy to decide.
So tell him to stop this salvation jazz thing,
For I am not one of these miserable sinners
The priest keeps rattling about every Sunday,
But a happy sinner who sure enjoys his glass of cool Guinness.
To me Heaven and hell are only two sides of the same coin,
Depends on how the priest puts it at your funeral service.
But for most of the time the verdict is that all our good souls
Will rest in eternal peace. I mean, what else can the priest say?
He only knows too well who pays his bills.

Charles doesn't know how to play fraud and to pray loud;
He detests the smell of spilled blood.
He reckons, as they say, no war is a good war.
Some wars are just, but all mothers' funeral tears are just too.
No death is a good death except Good Friday's death.
No gun is a good gun except the old cowboy's shot,
Safely on the telly, pointed at the Red Indian replica.

But you know Charles, the love-fear of his God; divine destiny
Far surpasses all that fine dinner offer, political desk, complete with house keys.
He is least impressed by his baby face smiling inside some journalist's camera.
Fame, money; don't even try. He says, "What more power does one need,
Save the Holy Spirit's dynamo grit-power resident inside of you?"

83. CHARLES OWOR
VILLAGE LAND

village land is the soil in which you are laid to rest.
so, we buried his body in Bungatira;
near the pine trees that we planted together with dad.
but then he defied the law of gravity
and flew away home.

84. MARGARET AKOT NGANWA

At the end of one's huddles race,
You lapel with roses, medals;
Losers too,
You would knight in case they faint.

Frightened nights, closing nights;
On balancing scales
You would phone, touch,
Just in case the scales
Would dip to last,
And lose forever.

85. LUKA LUGOYA

Stood on my noonday shadow
Till you rode off
Into the mirage horizon.
Impressions of our friendship
Stood, whelmed,
Like the noonday airs.
Then I said,
Good-bye.

86. ABNER MWAKA OWOR

You led my tender fingers
Through volumes
Of Leonardo da Vinci,
And together we charcoaled
Some genuine muscles,
Portraits of wrinkled skin,
And images of ancient war machines.
You said,
"Maybe, you'll become an inventor too."

You perfected my art-blood cells
Through more charcoal and pencil lines,
Song imitations of the grain-bird,
And history told by crackling fire.
Driving through the rugged ravines,
And hunting Saturday Elands
On the oxygen-rich plains of Kidepo,
We captured more charcoal lines of primeval landscapes.
You said,
"Son, maybe you'll become a writer too."

You studied Divine lines,
Like the Italian master studying twisting muscles.
I said,
"Maybe you need a revelation."

I prayed the Master Designer
Himself show you beauty beyond Pluto,
And sure to His Word,
Before I laid your withering fingers down,
You were shown Heavenly palaces
Beyond recapturing in charcoal or pencil.

87. THE CITY OF COLOURED LIGHTS
(ABNER MWAKA OWOR)

I was shown an empty throne
In the great congregation,
And a robe hung by its arm,
Loose.
I was shown the city of coloured lights,
Where flowers and carpets of greener grass
Sing the songs of the beloved.
And my winged guide
Turned to me and
Without a mouth opened
Uttered, "It's all yours."

I was shown my own mansion,
Furnished in royal,
Like interlocking pyramids; magnificent
Forms mind-boggling for earthly architects.

Then I floated back
To join my dying body,
Now a shell.
More determined,
I cried again and again,
"How can I miss that throne,
For me reserved, wear that robe?"
I am glad I was shown the city
Of coloured lights.

88. DAVID HEWITT

You remind me
Of the protocol angels
Who wing tired saints
To their crystal sea thrones.

89. DR. ALOO MOJOLA

You taught me zigzag thinking, eccentric,
Like men who frontier night horizons,
And to salute anti-plumline.
You said, "That helps
To create new brain cells
For one's vacuum nut."
Discussing Greek philosophy
Was common over coffee
At the Hilton Hotel,
And liberation theology too.
The waiter would say,
"Mind keeping your voice down, Sir?"
"That sounds like our high school teacher, Mister Myers,"
You would say.

90. MARGARET NGANWA
(TRUE GREATNESS)

True greatness
Is
When great people
Think
You are great.
When
Mean and low people
Think low
Of me,
I worry not
Because Margaret thinks
I am great.
If
You doubt me
Ask Sir Winston Churchill.

91. SHANNON TITO

Can we take your ruddy, cheery, young brother back to Canada with us?

Yes, since I am also going to Scotland, not knowing when and where I return.
Yes, where I come from one can have two fathers and two or more mothers.
No, if you are going to adapt him and he vanishes in the Canadian white snow.
As for my other siblings, I will steal them back into Amin's Uganda in the
    same way
I smuggled them out through the Pokot wilderness of Western Kenya.

Can we take your ruddy spirited young brother back to Canada with us?

Yes, if he takes with him my old box guitar. He is a better musician than I,
Maybe he will become the lead singer with the top Canadian gospel
    group, "Lifeline."
Maybe he will become a leading academic in the whole of the of the
    West Coast.
No, if you are not going to look after his soul the way Susan, his sister did.
No, if he is going to buy into some Arctic demon, become the first black
    Santa Claus.
Yes, if he is going to become worship and care group leader in his church there.

Don't worry how he fits into the Canadian life; we are equally worried
    about ourselves.
When we left Canada some eight years ago, became missionaries in Kenya,
There was only one black and white TV per home.
Now there is a coulored tube in every room, including what we call the little room.
We used to go to the church camp to escape the city concrete and willful stress.
Now they call it a carnal sin not to have at least sixteen channels of TV at camp.
We got too used to the Kenyan ways, where things happen when they happen,
And the smiling faces of market women, kindly carrying shopping baskets for you,
And the pastor saying, "Dance until you drop dead, for that is a better way
    of dying."

Can we take your ruddy faced young brother back with us to Canada?

Yes, if he is going to another family there to settle down and get the job done.
Become almost all to him in a foreign land: friend, sister, and mother.
Yes, if he is going to produce two lovely boys, Jermaine and Ashton,
One to become the first black Canadian Prime Minister,
And the other to excel in the multi-coulored global cog, like father like son.
Yes, if they will keep their marriage, as Mother will tell them on their
    wedding day.
No, if it will work as Western shopping, pelting away anything two
    months old.
Yes, if you will remain uncle "Super Dad" as we know you in Nairobi.

Can we take your fired up young brother back with us to Canada?

Yes, if he will become a bridge between White and Black, Rwenzori and
    the Rockies,
Championing the cause of peace as his future late brother Charles
    did, passionately.
Yes, if he will have three homes: one in Vancouver, one in Bali
    among Sea-Palms,
One in Amuru with peacocks patrolling the university's macadamia farms.
Yes, if he will have two fathers, two or more mothers, some white, some black.
No, if he will become a statistic gear in an automobile factory with nothing to
    show for it.
Yes, if he will complete his divine destiny, God's multi-coulored mandate
    to humanity.

92. ERN BAXTER

You drew
Ecclesiastical mansions
On molded walls,
Prayed up revelations,
Fixed horizons
On levelled eyes,
Raising hearts.

Immovable clergies
With obstinate hearts,
They wondered
Why new horizons;
Not new really,
But ancient truths
Camouflage in molded stones.

And so you laboured
To redraw clear mansions,
To untangle beams
Of future glories
That could be now.

Then I saw from a bird's view,
Saw from a worm's view,
I inspected its pillars
And proved your structure.
It hugs down well.

93. TIM TAKI

When you meet him
he will be breezing
tunes from Beethoven's "Pastoral,"
reading a post-graduate textbook
of astrophysics or something.

But then he was doodling a scene
from the Genesis flood,
with occasional verbals of Marion William's,
"I know a great Savior, don't you?"

"Are you Tim Taki?" I asked
"Taki with a k and i" he corrected,
finishing off the head of a croc.

94. THE TREKKERS

In the days of our youth,
We bibled the dusty tracks of Kenya
With our "Elka" sounds.
Twenty watts was good enough
For the Presbyterians
And the wattle school that shacked
At the end of the dusty tracks.
They would alter down their sins
In awful numbers.

We charged the coffee houses,
Prayer meetings with anointed electrons,
And Fred Ojiambo would say,
"Keep the Elka sound
At level thirteen
While I challenge these numbed heads
With evidence as true as me."

You could hear a pin drop then,
Even with the Elka at level thirteen,
In those days of our youth.

There was Tim Taki
At the lead mic,
Boni Adoyo, Kwame Rubadiri,
Grace Khamadi, Margaret Munano,
Their voices meeting hearts
like the melting sun.
Rhoda Ondeng's fair-faced renderings
Were fair to all church spires,
Until Sekou Rubadiri
Would distill in some Comodores,
Earth Wind and Fire,
Or any Motown sound.

Stringed were James Matagaro,
Martin Bando, and Fred Ojiambo
Doing their version of
"His name Is Jesus,"
Dougie solid on the bass guitar.
But there was Jack Odongo
And Paul Mpaayei on keyboards,
As if they invented the ivory scales,
And myself at the drums, palpitating
Like the day the Hebrew children
Crossed the Red Sea.

We pioneered
Afro-gospel electric sound,
Weaved in some black blood
In the "Amazing Grace" song.
Luckily, its composer was long dead.
Martin's guitar "wa-wa" sound

Peeved the hell out of the Methodists,
My triple para-dribbles on the drums
Waking up every Baptist's pew,
And the pastor at the African Inland Church
Paced up and down the aisle,
"I need to clear these strange electric gadgets
With our board of elders."

Electric gadgets indeed;
Our African American patron, Kathyrn Mbaathi, asked,
"And how will all these gadgets fit in my car,
Together with all of you 'Amazing Graces'?"
"As one thousand species of millipedes fitted in Noah's ark,"
I replied.

How pleasant it was
To serve the Lord
In the days of our youth.
Now I meet those wattle kids
Behind pulpits, awesome desks;
In offices that intimidate you
When the secretaries would bellow,
"Did you make a prior appointment, Sir?"
"No, Madam, but I electrocuted his dead cells
In the days of our youth,"
I would bellow back.

95. LAMAR OCITTI

Some are petal born;
Palmed,
With roses.
They twinkle.

96. MRS. CHRISTINE OWOR

you died with
your son
on your lips,
with THE SON.
whooping, wheezing
against hope
you could see,
touch your son.
but THE SON
was there.
and you said,
"Thank you."

97. GENERATIONAL FOUNDATIONS

Won't you get tired of saying,
"My mother used to say"?

98. PASTOR JAMES OCHOLLA

Like you,
If all saw me
Through the binoculars
Of the divine lighthouse,
Sailing smoothly over the waters
I would have long anchored in,
But then
I would have missed
The crashing rocky breakers,
And the surfing game.

99. CHARLIE BOLTON

Once you learn
To read his brain,
You'll understand
Why he made us dig
Granite holes
On acres of diamond.

100. BETTY OWOR ALLIMADI

Will I completely forget
The voice sound, tender,
The smile reflections,
And moan un-tapped echoes
That recede with the years?
Your audacity, urgency,
Clarioning the Great News,
That pulled even you,
A naughty school frock,
As if sure of your clock time,
To complete your errand quick.
I pray I remember always
The kind-firm face,
Face the great and small,
Beauty now reflected
In the ones who said, "Yes,"
To your urgent proclaim.

Betty Allimadi 1954–1984

101. **PASTOR SUSAN OWOR**

You taught me the ways of violent ripping prayers
That say, "Enough is enough; back with my stuff, all of it,
Paid in arears, interest attached, brimmed, running over."
Prayers that appertain to my destiny, divinely set,
But none buried in the cemeteries of the famous nobodies.

You taught me the ways of violent ripping prayers
That fist, "We got the power! The impossible made Him-possible."
Creating the same up-lift force that shuttled Him from the dead
So near to us; on our lips—that close, near our doorstep.
That prod, "Speak it; to your mountains!
They have to move, because they have to move."
Unlike presumptuous, naïve, guileful plots,
But a childlike faith that flouts theological chatter;
That says plainly, "We are children of the Palace."

You taught me the ways of violent prayers,
Prayers that earn dividends, life sized, in Jesus' name.
The proof: our crimson blood-dipped robes.
Business deals, bedridden, bed-bugged contracts bounce back to life,
Squandered nuptial circles slipped back in place,
Delinquent brats back at the doorsteps, weeping unchained.
Cancer, diabetics, arthritis, all have to curtsy out.

"No tenderfoot Ludos game," you said, it will be,
But agonizing, tarrying prayers, fluidless fasts; full armoured, geared,
Standing on the Word, seated celestially with the Son,
Using the awesome authority-baton passed at His ascent,
Commanding, kicking open ancient mulish gates, resisting all hell,
Trumpeting down divine fireballs, scorching to the roots
Charms, curses, causes, curtains, and covers,
Drawing bloodline between the past and the future,
Red eyed, charging, flashing two-edged sword, like Peter's
And all who embrace the ways of violent prayers.

OF POLITICS

Like those discussed
At the UN General assembly,
In university senior staff rooms,
In dark bar nooks
Away from heartless state ears

1. NORTH- SOUTH DIALOGUE

Pineapple slices
Are for daughters of kings;
Vanilla grows
Only in the sun.
Why give us
Plastic in return?

If ripe bananas
Didn't die young,
Their juice ferment into fuel
And could turn wheels round,
We'd all be happy men.

> *Black banana head!*
> *Who taught you thermo-dynamics,*
> *Who taught you Zoology,*
> *Taught you what is taught?*
> *Back with our capsules,*
> *Reincarnate David Livingstone*
> *To school you this talk,*
> *If you can.*

Blackboard; O black,
School talk indeed!

If Egyptian Pharaohs,
Black as they were,
Were not destroyed, erased
By Northern barbarians,
Now buried in triangles;
If they didn't feed on Nile cabbages,
Cabbages that floated from our source;
If they didn't feed on Delta garlic,
Who would have given you that school?

You despise our raw learning,
Our writing so uncooked.
The Japanese write
Like chicken feet; they do,
Yet they now rule
The electric world.

Were it not for the unfair
Powered gun unconquered,
We would be ruling
In Downing Street now;
Ten times... no, centuple kings,
And an Incas Colossus
Draped in Ibis feathers
For the Statue of Liberty;
This much is true.

Impudence of impudent mug-wump,
Australopithecus-Africanus,
Back to Olduvai Gorge,
Creeping, go.
You may be
The grandfather of us all,
But what marks your history
With celebrity

Apart from inventing cloves?
You try now to dress Lagos like Paris,
Only a Third World stench you get.
This much is true.

This much is true indeed.
To hell you go, UNEP;
To hell with your industrial chimney talk,
Global warming alibi.
Now is our turn
To pollute the Nile,
Chop the Amazon.

Go chop the Amazon,
To run your cabs
On black Amazon charcoal, if you can.
For us
We are on microwave.

Third World I am,
One with the Black;
You call me chapatti head,
Detest my dhal.
If you bombed Calcutta flat,
We will still be there,
Long grain rice feeding.
I don't need a locomotive
To climb the Himalayas,
The Sherpas do it barefooted.
I don't need Queen Mary
To teach me to design a sari.
All I need is towatch
The sun set
Over River Ganges.

Ah! River Ganges indeed.
I swear by ten floating corpses,
On River Ganges,
By a hundred I swear.
We climbed your Kilimanjaro
While you drank palm wine,
Timorous of touching its snow,
Lest you wake its guardian bee.
You can go worship Mahatma Gandhi,
Haile Sellasse, or whoever can wear a sari.
For us the cross is creed,
And Christ the King.

For us the cross is Creed,
And Christ the King too.
Egypt-Africa was Christianized before you.
If Lima, Cairo were to sneeze
And cough
Under some mad atomic dust
Will Paris, New York,
Or Lisbon live
To say the grace, ever?

If we pollute the Nile,
Will the fish in Crete
Swim with ease?

If you pollute the Nile,
No fish in Crete will
Swim with ease.
Manhattan was built
On Mandingoes digging free.
And Liverpool spins on, breathes on
Because we, together,
Dressed our wounds

With pieces of the Union Jack,
In the paddy fields.

2. PALM OIL TOPPING
(SONG OF AN ECONOMIC REFUGEE)

If only blazing sun and flooding rain
Didn't compete the huddles race,
And the hot Equator sun
Dehydrate our life-and-death cotton fields;
If only our fishes swam
Straight into tin cans,
Everything raw, exported raw.

> *I wouldn't be here*
> *Chewing this plastic cheeseburger,*
> *And buttery chicken*
> *That tastes like chipboard.*

If only mosquitoes had bites that blessed,
And tropical viruses novices,

> *I wouldn't be here*
> *Swallowing these myriad pills*
> *To keep my blood pressure*
> *Below the hospital bed.*

If only our politicians
Didn't fight over microphones,
Or use the barreled guns as walking sticks;
If only our State Houses were left
To post-colonial democrats,
Who have some fatherly genes; at least,

I wouldn't be here
Trying to fit into this maddening
Social jungle
That even spit at the word "mother."

If only they didn't make
All of us scribble servants,
Educated, jobless idiots,
Of long dead colonial desks,

I wouldn't be here
At this assembly line,
Trying to please
People who have long lost
The simple phrase,
"Thank you."

Just think of peppered okra sauce,
With palm oil topping,
Lipped inside a grass-thatched hut,
And rain bathing the tropical blades.
Just think of peanut-malakwang leaf
With smoked guinea fowl steak;
Goes well with Cassava-Millet bread,
Mixed five in eight.
Think of chilled passion juice
And fresh jackfruit,
Straight from the trunk,
The sun hitting you on the head
As if you abused its mother.

What would one need these vitamin-minerals
Tablet additives for?

Think of the sound of tom-toms,
As they pulsate through the African night,
And the moon agreeing with you
That joy is not the noise of seamless discotheques,
But the answering rhymes of innocent virgins,
And with the young and old bones alike,
At the Mzee Alipayo Oloya's village arena,
And the night owls in dark places,
Echoing the bass lines,
And the twittering beetles modulating
With the glow-worms, revealing
The secrets of ripe lovers
Among the Napier grass blades,
During the December love-months,

What would one look for
In a smoking, foul smelling night club?

Think of the sound of children
Playing the Lawala game,
And bathing babies crying of cold water.
Think of butterfly–coloured market women
Chattering away bundles of bananas and dried fish.
Think of un-orchestrated noise
In over packed Leyland buses
As they pass the colonial police station
In state of post-colonial disrepair.

A pawpaw ripe mother's breast
And her suckling child;
Never a public-bus disgrace,
But life spelled.

Recall those Saturday afternoons
At the Pece local stadium;

Football was not about technique and scoring
But style and agitating, master-poise;
How to dodge your mate till the women cheer,
And afterwards at Uncle Dwong's steak-house.
Think of Sunday morning with Pastor Maliko,
And the choirs with ten watt battered speakers,
But with real-size miracles walking
In Jesus' name,

Wouldn't you take the first plane home?
But then, I wish we had enough jobs to eat,
And our politicians
Didn't fight over microphones,
Or used barreled guns as walking sticks.

3. BRIGHT RED MORANS

Sorry,
I didn't learn
Much Swahili.
There are many foreign Pelicans
Who have laid a million eggs
On your land
Who can't even pronounce,
"Mbwa Kali."
So I guess it doesn't matter.

I'm sorry;
I don't know much
Kalimba thumbing,
Rhythm response. I am Caucasian;
I only came to bathe in the sun,
See wild giraffes,
Take red African pictures
For my wife
Of Maasai Morans palisading

Like the Leaning Tower of Pisa.

Sorry, had to leave
Without a word of farewell.
By the way,
The part I also loved too
Was sipping cane juice
At the Karen Hotel,
While watching the sun set
Over the Ngong hills.

4. THE SOLAR LINE

Chant, "Mandela! Mandela!" like Nyerere, Kwame Nkrumah.
Fist Amanza! Amanza! Shout, "Uhuru! Uhuru! Free at last!"
These statue marathon pace makers, first batons in the triple race.
What precipitates you free, present leaders, yet you feed not, suckle not your
     own kin?

Rather read Mandela's brain; he recalled those Boers, white water bucks,
     back home,
To co-habit a single humanity, pump sense into one another.
True, they palisade unashamed, embezzled, tricked old chiefs to sign
     misread treaties,
Smashed and ground ancient foundries, charred black our bark clothes.
But antibiotics, metal paths, and blackboard chalk they placed too on our laps.
Those independence fathers persevered, sacrificed their very bowels.

Look! You baggers, sway, trickle drips from your parvenu chalets,
And call it community alms, social obligation. Even Boy Scouts do it better,
Imitate British Lords' tea drinking, without a drop of imperial blood,
Bank in their banks, without a penny filtered back. Damned race you are.
Rather model Gaddafi, defying all odds and fend for your own people.

Revile not Idi Amin, Omar Bongo, Mobuto Ssese Seko,
Or count yet another African coconut, messing up the oven manuals,

Crowding us all, under the solar line, for the price of deflated cotton.
The Bongos are long dead, their wealth vaulted safe in European vaults.
It takes only one man, dreaming aright, to turn the tired tide around.
Rwanda's Kagame is doing it; Ghana's Cocoa-something has achieved it.
If you doubt me, take a flight to Singapore, observe for yourself;
Skyscrapers sing to each other, and cranes compete in the night.
We started the huddles race on a uniform colonial line, singing our anthems;
Now our songs are songs of intoxicated vultures, perched to skel-
    eton landmarks.
In the governor's days, prevailed at least a hospital bed per soul.
Now, three nurses bed-bug under one hospital bed,
And doctors share their gloves with overfed roaches,
Sleep on the operating tables, their prized tea, yellow-ochre water.
One could barter a goat or two for school dues, buy a Raleigh bicycle, then.
Now we all eye that election coin dished, to vote their Mitsubishi cars.
Desert Emirates started as desert Emirates, peddling camel hump merchandise,
Now they claim all world firsts, including the greenest grown cucumber.
Its leader an un-schooled Bedouin Tented Arab, who got his act together.

He created all equal. Rearrange, realign and get your acts together.
Why confess we are a mixed-up genre, fallacious, insidious boffins?
Look! From Lagos to Mombasa the stench the same, the jammed wheels.
Acclimatized, living in clutter, jumping Third World un-gagged canyons.
Accursed breed. Damned? He raises curses, grievous maladies.
Though guilty of bartering our own blood to Arab slave masters,
He's not the cosmic sergeant major. Will pardon, starting pot-bellied chiefs;
Enthralled, entranced by European beads, amusing mirrors and barreled guns,
Like neo-colonial chiefs, you dish virgin soil to soiled, oblong-nosed investors,
To build guilt apartments, buy Japanese wheels; you call that eco-
    nomic growth.
No. That is not Gross Domestic Product; it's Gross Domestic Profanity,
Punishable by subdued un-anesthesia castration, even by ICC dictate.
Why reprimand these honorables? Let them eat weevils with prison rats.
Only absolve yourself imagining yourself but a cursed race.

Why buy base Chinese plastic that last only two days. Mould your own.
"We have no resources, micro-chip," you cry. It's only imagination you lack.
Visualize a million dollars from foreign pinholes, clicking some ugly chimps,
Million dollars from oblong noses come to breathe your virgin air.
If you can't manufacture laptops, then for goodness sake, make your rap top.
This Kwasakwasa music, if it's that good, sing your way to Japan or some
    new town.
"We have no resources, micro-chip," you say. Its only mind block you have.
Don't you know that an African American will pay all his guts can gut
To buy one square inch of dead African soil and call it home?
Why moan? Sudan is semi rock, Burkina Faso is semi rot, Tanzania is
    semi rough.
Learn from Botswana, for goodness' sake. They carve sirloin steak on late
    rite soil.
If you can't grow Pawpaws, then harvest Gum Arabic that grows wild on any
    rite soil.
If you doubt me, ask any Israeli how they rule the citrus world on semi
    dead rock.

If you don't know what lies beneath that dry face, then ask any colonial map.
It giggles as you scuttle—stupid, grappling for string-tied foreign aid.
Oil flows your sub-terrarium streams, like tributaries to any tributaries;
Would make Colonel Gaddafi run for thirtieth term as African King.
Diamond, stretches from Angola to Mozambique in scintillating seams,
Reducing Buckingham Palace vaults to miniature cassones.
Cotton grown even in Sahel sand would reproduce multiple Liverpools.
This time we'll furnish our Palaces, Byzantine, with Congo teak,
Hand-carved statues of our independence fathers with ebony precision.

Still wail, "We Africans are dense, thick like our cotton-bale hairs?"
Go to Microsoft and NASA, see whether we are only cleaners, janitors there.
Haven't you yet heard Olara Otunnu addressing scribbling pens at the UN?
They develop by agglomerate snowballing din, not by superior intelligence.
If you doubt me, ask any first-year economics student; of these you fear white.
You too can pen and dust blackboards to unimaginable awesome levels.

These certificates earned, are they interior design knick-knacks, to wall hang,
Or to turn wheels round, blade grass to grain and celebrate daring
    dreams achieved?
The pharaohs who built the sphinxes, were they not blue-black like you
    and me?
If you doubt me, ask Ali Mazrui, then burn all those fib European
    history books.
Don't worry about the colour of your skin; someone has to be black anyway.
Remember one day people will fight to be born in the Congo.

Still worshiping, adulating those African gods and demi-gods?
You pride it culture, "This is mother Nile, this is spirit Shaka-Zulu."
You complete all your school tasks then park your four-wheels under a
    baobab tree;
Consult Mother Nile and her underwater demons to give you sweatless wealth,
Lay your woes before leopard-skinned witches, hypnotized by calabash sound.
What did you chalk blackboards for, burn school candles for?
Remember your Sunday school rhyme, "Came He to open blind eyes,
Black or white, save from hell, taught or untaught," so save yourself a trip to
    the baobab,
Rearrange, realign, get your acts together. Listen to your brain, it's
    mighty clever.
Medieval Europe came to hard terms, was the beginning of their beginning.
I perceive, though, sadly their grandsons now melt before medieval art,
    Eastern deities;
Signal beginning of their end, their social and self-solicited crunch.
With grace we can begin our beginning, evade the social melt down, self-
    made crunch.

5. CENTRIFUGAL ENGINE
(FIFTY-YEAR DEVELOPMENT PLAN)

Make them poor, patched, lined behind the poverty line;
Let them gasp for air, scrum down like rugby game,
Fight for that coin flipped in the air; a Gaddafi type generosity,
Heedless of coins tucked in some European vaults.

Then they will vote us yet another term;
Singing victory songs at our champagne popping,
Believe the single coin was indeed flipped down from Heaven.
Then they will believe in the "limited resource law,"
And "prosperity out-burst derived inflation."

Teach them nonsense, write nonsense curriculums,
Of homeless history, white social psychology, and dead mathematics,
Straight from some PhD. thesis, clever workshop handouts.
Make them educated idiots, masters of pure mathematics
That won't job any job, innovate another canned coin.
This is PhD: Permanent Head Damage.

Then they will keep to the streets, shoe heels tar-braised flat,
Knocking on every white-coloured door, believe in that cocktail
job promise.
Then they will come running back to us, gasping for air,
Use their own certificate papers to clean our toilet holes.

Keep the centrifugal engines on, coagulating the fair ones to the centre,
And chaff at the edge; circulating at the speed of cosmic madness,
Just to remain within the same milky-way, never touching the real milk.
Emphasize again the laws of limited resource supply, keep the inflation
   rate stable
By foiling every scum head breaking loose from the rugby scrum.

Then we will remain at the top, ruling from the only room at the top.
But were there more rooms, we can't fill the top with every scum head,
Straight from the rugby scrum, smelling like two-day dead tilapia fish.

Divide tribe against tribe, region against region; imperial planners' way:
Kikuyus against Luos, Northern Luyas against Central Luyas.
Let the Baganda think they are superior because they saw the first white,
Had kings who ruled like Western monarchs, for better, for worse,
And the Acholis because they led the Kings African Rifles in Burma and India,
Each called only by thirteen-digit numbers, fighting a homeless war.
Let every oblong nosed Tutsi, any fair-skinned black think they are closer
     to Caucasian,
Matabele against Ndebele, though both black monkeys, as known in
     some circles.

Then we would have created a perfect society, a board game as easy
     as Ludo.
Then they will be at each other's throats, fighting for that flipped coin;
A delayed discourse, good for the election day, a false state of emergency,
While we drink toasts at the African State House sun-downer gardens.

Bring them out of the rural areas, in hoards, bus-loads, train-loads, foot-loads,
Let them say their last vows to their grandmothers, to ancient clan-hills
     so dear,
A last gaze at the family graves, wishing them good luck, a fair trial at the
     city courts.
Let them give a last stare at the corn fields, so faithful in the years past
But now too dehydrated to feed mouths and compete with our mega trac-
     tored fields.
Slot in a few coloured light in the cities, disco sounds and prostituting thighs.

Then they will scoot to the cites in bus-loads, train-loads, and foot-loads,
Cling to lamp posts like Nsenene grasshoppers attracted to death lights.
Then they will all run to those construction site wheelbarrows, paid
     chicken wings;

Forever be grateful for the wheelbarrows, then stare at the dehydrated
corn fields,
Forever grateful their corn fields are at last sold, can complete the belated
bride price.

"If you can't beat them, join them." Let that be the song of new and old
M.Ps alike.
Let them be at each other's throats, trying to get to the centre; centre of things;
Abandon all pseudo-political rhetoric and second-degree type socio-politi-
cal debate,
And cling only to the one political lamp post, the one that feeds their
family mouths.

Then we would have created a perfect parliament, perfect socio-politi-
cal house;
Then they will vote us another term in office, vote themselves another
term too;
Singing victory songs at our champagne popping, giving cocktail
job promises
To slit skirt college girls come too, for the cocktail champagne
popping game.

Slot in random developmental projects: new roads that run to no-run places,
Bridges that join vacuum to vacuum, solar panels on old colonial tin roofs,
Schools that, by any mean dictator, should have existed there anyhow,
Miniature agricultural demonstration gardens squeezed within tropical
bramble bush,
Mega rural water schemes that well out five cupfuls a day, and the
Minister himself
Will come to open the project, the IMF regional representative seated by.
They will all clap to the two cupfuls, and traditional ladies dance to a work
well done.

We would have created a good report back to the World
Bank nerve-centre;

Good theme for yet another seminar workshop, "Sustainable
Reconstruction Pillars."
And they would come to the workshops in hoards, dressed in second
hand suits,
Endorse funding for another Sustainable Reconstruction Pillar and follow-
up seminar.

And life will go on in this our blessed continent, where the sun shines freely,
Paying no rent for the rain, the rivers that flow unchecked up to the
    Mediterranean Sea,
The tropical blades that grow, die, without anyone saying, "Hey, wait
    a minute."
And life goes on, everyone happy. We are happy at the centrifugal centre;
They are happy at the edges, pushing bucketfuls of sand on construction sites.
Otherwise the traditional ladies in bright colours won't be singing our
    victory songs.

OF CONFLICTS

which only your
Solomon brain-lobe
can solve.

58. SAMPLE S'S

Salted salt
Sweetened sugar
Scottish spirits
Sumptuous sludge
Smelly skunk
Saddening sanitarium
Scientific scrap
Sleepy salamander
Substitute sanctuary
Substitute sex
Senseless sarcasm
Shameless Scrooge
Structured scruffiness
Subversive science
Sermon-snore

Scantily slumber
Stupid smoker
Sinister smirk
Scholastic schlock
Sanctimonious sacrilege
Senseless sacrifice
Sadistic satisfaction
Subjugate settlement
Savage saga
Senseless scatter
Scaring sarcoma
Sinful solar system
Segregate socialite
Satanic scheme
Swollen scrotum.

59. HORSE FROM A RATTLE SNAKE

next time
you stumble upon two
breast-bulbs ripening,
on the non-return street
to Sahel,
plagiarized,
decoyed,
next time
you linger on silky thighs

beckoning,
and pirate lips glazed;
red as the Eden's apple,
ponder
your vista:
death
walking
double limbs.

60. LIVING WATER

When your thirst is water
It's trivial.
When the thirst you thirst
Is hid from His unsensual angels,
And your senses sense it,
"Obey your thirst!"
Before you do ...
Thirst still!

When the pride of life,
Be it propelling appetite,
Further still,
Call to astound,
Exfoliate
Those you reckon dehydrated,
Deprived of sap,
Before you do ...
Don't!

When the monkey looks,
And money unlocks
The urgent reservoirs of want,
Exudes power, paraded;
Land you on crystal atrium,
Hides your nakedness

At the cat-walk game,
Before you skip ...
Split!

But you perceived well,
Power is a fermenting agent,
The love for money,
The worm resident side
Of the same apple,
Merely turns to paralyzing odium.
The very love once caressed
The tale of the mistaken angels
And their dilapidated disciples.
Sagacity: Wonder
Whether this sweet caress,
Exacting thirst once vowed
To die for, is worth dying for.
But before die ...
Live!

61. AND THAT'S THE DIFFERENCE

For you, tomorrow is tomorrow;
You predict its coming
As if you were God.
For us, tomorrow is any other day
But yesterday and today.
Your meetings start on a dotted time;
Ours start when they start,
And end when they end.
The minutes of your meetings are recorded
With blackened ink;
Ours are sung by women;
They last for generations.
That's why you dare not speak carelessly
In the council of elders.

For you, no means no, and yes means yes.
For us, no means
The matter is worth considering,
And yes
Means the matter is worth considering.

For you,
Your uncle is your uncle;
For us, one's uncle is one's father too,
And has the right to discipline you on the spot.
One's uncle's wife is one's wife,
Don't ask me how.
She is the one who simulates for you the wedding night.
Every clansman or woman
Is a brother or sister.
You lie with one
At the price of sacrificing a black goat.

For us, sex and making love
Are words
Spoken only in awesome places.
For you,
Even your kids
Know how to count a woman's moon-days.

For you,
A beautiful woman
Is bred on a bean at dinner
And resembles that dehydrated ghost
That appears on the television,
You call a Hollywood Queen.
For us,
A beautiful woman
Has a dimple on her cheeks,
A gap in her teeth,

With a smile as white as the egret,
And a waist that hails from East to West.

For you,
Marriage is based on love;
For us, marriage is based on marriage
And rarely fails,
Except if the inside of the woman's womb
Was licked by a bewitched leopard.
For us, a child
Is a gift from God;
Its seed comes from a man's waist,
And has the blessing of elders.
For you, they are necessary evils
Who even stand when elders sit.

For us, when a neighbour
Asks you for one or two tomatoes
To feed his children for the night,
You give him enough to last
A week or so.

For you, when a senior speaks,
You look straight into their eyes,
For what would you be hiding if you didn't?
For us, when a senior speaks,
We dare not look into their eyes,
For it is a sign of disrespect and dishonour.

For us, wealth and dignity are measured
By the number of cows, wives, and children you have,
And how many clansmen can stand with you
In the fight,
And whether when you speak in the council of elders,
Even children refrain from passing out gas.

For you, being wealthy is easy.
It's having a big car, big bank account,
Big; everything big.
But who has ever been buried by money?

For you, a friend is the business diary
You consult when the sailing is green.
With a true friend
You can even share the abdomen of the
Delicious white ant.
A true friend is like your mother;
He is the only one who can tell you
That you went to the toilet
And forgot to use the toilet paper.

For you, when a man dies,
He is dead.
For us, he has only gone
To join his forefathers;
Who sure can see you
When you sleep with your neighbour's wife,
Or when you abuse your own wife
As if she has now not become
The mother of your offspring;
Now your own mother too.

God, to you, is only a dispenser of wealth,
The money purse, which has long left
The Western breadbasket.
But to us, money comes, money goes;
It is God who provides.

You can predict exactly
The month, the hour a child is to be born.
For us, counting their number alone

Is a sacred exercise.

We admire your inventions;
We understand when you travel in the air
By aeroplane,
You can even go to the toilet there.
You mean you have no respect for God,
Who lives in the skies?

62. SMELL OF SULFUR:
THE NORTHERN UGANDA CONFLICT

*The Northern Ugandan conflict between the rebel group The Lord's Resistance
Army, led by their notorious and elusive leader Joseph Kony, and the Ugandan
government of Yoweri Museveni, lasted more than twenty years (1987–2007).
Most of the population of Acholiland were either interned and lived in squalor in
government camps or killed! Children in the region captured by the rebels were
used as child soldiers or sex slave for the rebels' army based in Northern Uganda
and Southern Sudan. Those children who were not capture (nicknamed "Night
Commuters") had to seek shelter in urban areas like Gulu or Kitgum, sleeping
on the street at night before returning to school or their homes in the morning.
The smell of sulfur or gun power, the smell of military conflict, was everywhere in
the region.*

Conflict, insurgence, civic arrest, disturbance-smoke ... any name.
It was suckling women sheltering in squirrel barrows, between potato mounds;
Emaciated babies gagged to silence with the night, laid amidst hay.
Stray hounds did learn those days that with the first bullet sound,
It was time to break camp, leave whatever bone till God knows when.
Schoolgirls wished they were less beautiful, lest they become first target—
Fought over wives for Kony's commanders, other commanders
Carry un-aimed babies on their backs, automatic gun in one hand,
A ten-kilo life and death luggage in the other, and commanded, "Run, fast!"
Invisible children trek to town evening by evening, sleep inside car tires;
Boy soldiers, baby demons, blood hungry, taught to eat human intestines,

Anything school, pen ended, if lucky, captured and returned to Gulu,
Become construction site plastic buckets and gaze at the setting sun.
At best, die a security guard in Kampala, paid chicken wings.

Was it war between Southern and Northern Uganda?
Was it the old political school: neutralize, humiliate, control, exfoliate?
A clever castrametation, counter castigation, and final castration?
Was it the North fighting the South, the rest smiling at the butchering,
A subtle retaliation, a monkey-clap at an enemy agony pander?
Whatever form, it was Uganda at stake, the Centre, East suffering alike.
The national flag flies one, prays one, independent colours stand:
One boasts a lighter complexion, superior tribe, all black;
Some live under tiled roofs, all live under the yellow sun,
One pinched once, others pinched thrice, the same blood flows red.
The peace crane surrounded by white nectar, never to be replaced by the bee;
However sweet the honey, however sweet the stolen saccharine.

Was a war between stupidity gunned and intelligence abused?
A meaningless butt; most loosing, those winning only in delayed spit.
Not a district claimed, not a town captured, no manifesto written.
Was chalk less brutes hoping they can rule and entire country,
Address the United Nations on global warming, engine an economy.
The LRA teaming guerilla fighters; man-like chimps, chimp-like men.
Old men fought with little girls over weekly shame rations in the IDP camps.
Children born within the Sorghum years ignorant of the taste of domesti-
    cated milk;
The tallest fully-grown soul down to four feet tall, too dwarf to pass the
    primary exams,
But thank God the war is over, though they didn't see much chalk,
Only the reverse side of the black board, written: "Twenty years of bananas."
Young men, young ladies roamed the grass-thatched cities, searching for hope.
For sure they found it: in crude gin, illicit sex, konfu video halls, and Hell
    In View/aids.

NGOs regret the war is over; end of seminars, end of reports sent abroad,
Reports sent back from abroad, workshops; that means money,
Apartments built on ghost payroll and vacuum rations.
Don't cry the war is over, that you only got up to the ring beam.
Elite children study abroad, wives shop in the air, mouths wiped with
    dollar bills.
Expanded dimension: war tickled the Arab Northern Sudan, fanned
    more greed,
Caused a ripple in the Christian Sudan; controlled with desert dagger,
Blocked anything sane, paralyzed anything sublime; marching forward.
Oil rich, mineral loaded South Sudan threatened; America jumps in action.
Suddenly, young altar boy from Odek is the centre of interna-
    tional controversy.
Rome smells the possibility of this Catholic boy, Joseph Pattini
    Anantiano Kony,
Becomes Uganda's first Catholic president; excellent script for an action-
    packed movie.
But how didn't astuteness allow for an earlier end than twenty years?

It was spirits and voodoos in command, dearth "Abiba" eagles, demon perches,
Late nite stone grenades exploding, armored convoy vans thumped to shards;
Was Shea-nut oil bullet proof protection smear; wouldn't dare try it on, were
    I you.
Was true, unless you are ignorant of demon power and prefer it clean
    and scientific.
Bees, GPS guided by witches, sting at will, at full buzz, saturated the landscape.
Both armies resort to mutual bewitching and exorcism; compete
    at wickedness,
Bring yours from Nigeria, we'll bring our witches from India; more daunting,
Unaware it's a losing game when two devil cousin brothers fight their
    happy game:
Their triple mandates uniform; kill, kill, kill, the side of the slaugh-
    ter irrelevant.
These things you don't pen, table in parliaments, present to the ICC,

Don't quote me either. We are all educated, edulcorated Westerners, aren't
    we all?

Foot distance covered unfathomable: Soroti to Torit, From Kotido
    to Pakwach,
Not on tarmac, A1 motorways, but whiskey savannah bramble bushes, thistles,
At demonic speed, they dodged rolling tanks, wired rubber, fool traps.
Kony's baby soldiers paralyzed the landscape, silenced all bird songs.
Every flowing blood forced into displaced camps, potato mounds become
    hiding booths.
"Follow us if you must," they said in Acholi. "Your shit will turn into mud."
The National army was after them too. "Rape another girl and you will
    smell sulfur."
Twenty sorghum years: no one winning, all losing except masonry
    bricks staking.
A battle between stupidity gunned and intelligence abused, a state of orga-
    nized chaos.
Thank God the spirit filled Christians had to take charge, prove who truly is
    in charge,
When peace talks became peace jokes, armoured tanks laid to rest, inept to
    count the dead:
Annihilated, burnt down Kony's formidable stronghold at Te Got Atto,
    near Gulu;
Criss-crossed another of his demon strong booths in Sudan, with the blood
    of Jesus,
Waved the gritty old book at the father of all lies, "No more touch one of my
    little ones."
And that was the end of the war, end of dearth Abiba eagles and
    demon perches.
Peace talks had become peace jokes, armoured tanks laid to rest, inept count
    the dead;
Kony is now safe and dry in Central Africa or wherever, pollinating
    another evil,
But as we all know, devils never die; they only relocate, like children
    cartoon characters.

Internally displaced camps rose like white ant cities upon the landscape;
Years of Bananas, but a new energy created, a new synergy; bitter-sweet taste.
Bananas indeed, but even wild Latembe bananas, when ripe, hungry, one can
    eat still.
Something conversable must permeate outside this infectious, insidi-
    ous malady.
All sinister wars distill into sizzling rays of hope, that is a global law:
Little displaced camp paraffin kiosks turned into neighbourhood shops;
Stone settled peasant farmers, who had no need of town, no need of school,
Comfortable cattle herders who cared less about city lights, running water,
Were rooted out of their two-legged stool acclimatization, had to beg at the
    IDP camps,
All had to learn words like: ration, rape, rice, routine, regulate, readiness;
Yes, readiness to turn from fourth world to third world, at least.
Nucleated settlements: concept of all concepts for any civilization re-birthed.
Land freed to breathe, opened all blind eyes to potential of mecha-
    nized farming.
Many had to run into exile in Europe, Australia, America, and Tongo;
    Tongo land
Now are Acholi-English, Lango-Swiss, Teso-Belgians, Acholi-Acholi Germans;
The delicious 'Tugu' palm fruit scattered in anger only propagates more
    further afield.
Nagasaki and Hiroshima bombed flat only made the Japanese rule the elec-
    tric world.
Invisible children out of the car-tire blankets now like cockroaches out of
    nuclear clouds.

63. ETERNAL LEGS

is she worth
going to Hades,
for fifteen minutes
of pleasure like Heaven?

is she worth the
un-blessed hour

for a visit to eternity lost,
my friend?

consider fifteen
vapour-lost tickings
of pleasure like Heaven,
my friend.
ever sat on red-white coals,
swallowed wet overfed worms?
ponder squillion
hooked ones oozing out of
hell's cavity lunch?

still dreams
of your peri-wedded gal
bathing stack naked
in the rain?

"yes,"
he said,
"she's got legs,
I mean legs,
like props to
atoning Heavens."

64. SAND DUNES OF KIDEPO

Loved to walk
Those wild sand dunes
Of Kidepo river bed,
Risk the river water wall
Advance its shield
Like merciless palisade;
Outcome of a distant storm.

Loved to lie there on my back,
Watch cumulous clouds merge
And unmerge, ad hoc.
Loved to play those uncertain dunes;
Play with salt-less beach sand,
A test of one's controlled stupidity,
Publishable in the annals
Of educated psychopaths, buffoons
Receive a certificate for outwitting death.

Loved to hope against hope
The sure winding rivers,
Bending suddenly, expose not a lost cub
Nor a barreled tribal warrior;
Those days of AK 47s,
Which may welcome you
With a triggered smiling smoke.
But still, I loved to walk, play
Those wild sands of Kidepo.

65. BRAIN DANCE

You smiled; the game was over.
You scored three goals to one.
You stole meat after ten—was sweet,
Like red wine sparkling free,
Running down smooth.

Nothing like a touch of feminine curve,
Was powerfully sweet,
And apparently offended no one
Except your fingertips.

But wonder now,
Was it worth kicking God in the face?
Was glad your repentance wrought release

And true reflections of life as should be.

Nothing, you see now like a sea of crystal,
Calm before the jury divine,
When you reflect your face,
Not the head of a sphinx you see.

Nothing like a dip in the cool;
Only for a drink of life,
When you wet your palms
Together with Pilate's:
Yours clean through and through.

Meat stolen after ten was sweet,
Like red wine sparkling free,
Running down smooth,
Only turning to gall sucking worms,
Making one's brain dance with elephants
With pink ears flapping in tune.

As the Sunday school rhyme says,
"It always pays
To let the cookies cook
Until it's properly cooked
And have properly with tea."

66. HOMEOPATHY

Sex on the infant lip:
Rhyme it, demystify it,
It's elementary biology,
It's semen, it's fallopian tubes.
What else?

Sex; blackboard, inked,
More sex reel to reel.

I saw it through the eye
Of chalk and overhead projector.
The boys liked it;
The girls hid behind their giggles.
They all said,
"Sir, we have understood,
Except this thing, love."

The medical students dissected, discovered
The fallopian tube does indeed exist,
It's chromosomes, hormonal balance, what else?
They, now men, liked it;
The ladies hid behind their giggles,
And they all said,
"Yes, Prof. we have all understood
Except this thing, love."
But then he said,
"Mine is only to help you play it safe."

So they tried it
On the student single bed;
The men liked it,
But didn't seem to get enough of it.
The ladies weren't too sure
It was as beautiful as the inks say it.
They felt painfully cheated
Of their wedding gowns;
Their last secret laid bare.

But then as the Prof. said,
"Mine is only to condom you
Into sterile sex.
Love and lab tests
Are yours to discover."

They tried it yet again
On the student single bed.
The ladies wanted more of love,
Less of sex;
The men said, "Love—well,
That is a mirage dream,
Lost the day
We first lipped the word 'sex'
In the Nursery school."

67. WARDROBE LIKE HIS

Stage poise	- Pro-frog,
Stage locomotion	- Clumsy,
Rhythm and bounce	- No sex appeal,
Pulpit manner	- Devoid of charm or calm,
Mike control	- un-coordinated,
Presence	- demandingly cheap,
Demeanor	- magnetically soft,
Enthusiasm	- misplaced,
Time management	- nil.
Projection	- perfectly awful,
Voice	- monotone, squeaks,
Diction	- comical,
Vocabulary	- terribly limited,
Wardrobe	- lamentingly arcane,
Stature	- lacks altitude.
Sermons content	- sparingly challenging,
General direction	- three sixty degrees,
Attitude	- excellent,
Theological training	- three more years will do him good,
Bible knowledge	- good,
General knowledge	- constricted,
Jesus part	- over emphasized,
Anointing	- N/A.

Education,	- upper Kindergarten,
Referral	- deceased friend,
Curriculum vitae,	- scanty,
Air mileage covered	- ten metres,
Travel sickness	- Malaria,
Table etiquettes	- requires urgent attention,
Team playing	- recommendable,
Cultural ambience	- ample panel beating necessary,
Social background	- mysterious,
Blood lineage	- non-red,
Overall assessment (-5 to +5)	(- 4)
Conclusion	- resembles Apostle Peter.

68. UNTIL YOUR OWN NIGHT

Pending your graduation:
Virtues internalized,
Limbs mortified, abased,
Settling them, unremitting,
Close, on the night coach,
To tempted land,
Leaning their sleepy heads
On your sleepy shoulders,
Hankering, lustfully.

69. SLIDING INTO SECOND LOVE

When you begin to find it easier
To use the English Common Prayer Book,
The William Barclay's Bible Commentary,
Than getting it first hand from the Wind,
When you begin to congratulate yourself
For out-growing those charismatic experiences,
Tambourine banging, controlled chaos,
You would have left your first love.

When you begin to look trimmed,
Proper, painfully clean, envy the way
Those elders parade themselves navy-blue
In the church's first row, soft row,
Than desire the seat of a bond-slave
In the house of the Lord,
Then you are sliding into second love.

When you begin to wish
You too should have gone to Bible College,
And can use words
That can only be understood
In their original Greek and Hebrew,
Insist that the computer inserts
All your credentials one by one,
Behind your town-petrified name,
You are firmly into second love.

You are sliding into third love
When you begin to fight for
Who owns and controls the church,
Into fourth love
When you begin to draw anointing
To demonstrate power and authority
From the devil himself.

70A. HOME LOVE BAROMETER

You are sliding into third love
When you begin to ask the wife for just one thing
She ever learnt from her mother.
Into fourth love,
When you begin to reserve that flower
For her funeral.

70. I BELIEVE

I believe in God;
Father Almighty,
He's the only true God.
I thoroughly detest the worship
Of ancestral spirits,
Any form of magic craft,
White or black.
But what can a man do
If they want their business to flourish?

I believe in Jesus Christ.
He was a true prophet;
A good man.
Those Roman brutes
Surely don't deserve the Vatican
For a reward.

I believe in the Bible;
In it are words of wisdom,
And surprisingly in it
Are handy business tips;
Helps though to place it
Under your pillow
When the business is going crazy.

I am a Christian
Because I am neither a Hindu nor Moslem.
I believe in hell,
Because there sure must be a spot
For folk like Idi Amin and Hitler
To meet, share notes.
But for me, I go to church;
Ensure my entrance into heaven
And expect a decent funeral service.

Heaven, yes, ticket purchased,
But imagine me playing a harp,
Wearing a robe, whiter,
And chanting, "Holy, holy, holy,"
For the rest of eternity.

I go to church
Because every good Christian
Ought to go to church.
It is the place to rub shoulders
With the who-are-who's of the town.
Otherwise, church is a dead
And lifeless place.
Any case, tell me, what does one do
On a Sunday morning?
I'd rather listen to that preacher
Rattle on some irrelevant topic
Like the pros and cons of abortion,
Than have my wife bore me with
The latest formula
For hand and body lotion.

71. THE BEAUTY OF ZIG-ZAG

An ecclesiastical spire
Heaves out of a dome-hill,
Your steps, as they lead you on,
Heaves back into its sheath,
As if to play peek-a-boo
With your brain.

A goodly hamlet
Emerges out of a col.
Is your destiny in sight?
Fading, you zigzag on;
It's a welcoming

Melodrama suspended.
Surpasses the comfort
Of a prairie highway,
Destiny always in view,
But like chasing
The home of a rainbow.

Was a pity
You missed the corner café
That serves coffee,
With free semolina cookies,
Two turns away.

Faster then now you go;
A deer jumps out of a vacuum.
Was good you weren't asleep.
Yask! Could have cursed.

Down the green,
Over the trouted streams,
Left to the wooden trail;
Evil trunks they gaze,
Back and down right,
Your goodly hamlet out again.
Blast! "No through road!"
Back to junction T
Try again.

72. SONGS OF THE SEAGULL

You can fool your head,
Let it believe red
Was born out of blue,
But you can't fool your heart
To smile in the dark,
For it lives with God.

Learn to fly in the dream,
Stop the minute hand with a grin,
Visit a medium, pursuing solace,
But you'll return home
With a few more demons
Giggling on your back,
"Cured, cured, you are free!"

Yes, nothing like a dream,
That you were singing with the stars,
Praising till they remember dawn;
Nothing like a hymn on your lips
First thing in the morning;
It makes you agree with the rising sun,
With the songs of the sea gulls,
That all your debts are paid in full,
And that it's not worth
Crossing swords with God.

73. URBAN CREAM

Three life members approving, finally you made it.
We burnt gas, three gallons to the mile,
To attend our inaugural A.G.M,
Meet His Worship the Mayor,
And the men that made our town tick.
The night sailed smoother than we thought,
But we all agreed business was low,
And the slum improvement scheme must delay.
All nodded, "Yes, it presupposes an alternate course,"
And then went on to exchange manuals
For our new Japanese metals parked outside.

We all clapped to the Christmas tree
That was meant to cheer no one
Save the Salvation Army.

The night sailed on smoother than we thought;
Grins rehearsed, over rehearsed,
Speeches written only to fatten one's filing cabinets,
Ladies grouped into their vogue little corners,
Discussing metropolitan fashion and
Who is sleeping with whom,
By the latest video library.

Then suddenly one must go; exit less colourful,
Disgusted, disappointed, and all other Ds,
Together with the smell of sherry and ladies' cologne
Driving you crazy.
But what can one man do?
At least they are doing something
And have their fun and networking.

74. POISONOUS BARREN NEPTUNE

Love to meet You there ...
The wheeled metal,
It rolled off my love,
Was in a coma, agony finale—
Love to meet You at the answering ...
He failed to nod to our benediction.

They spend billions, scoop a cupful
Of inoperable gray lunar rock.
Pluto, Neptune that are larger,
Are barren, breathe poisonous fumes,
Evaporate you even before you start.
Are they worth the search?

Little Johnny, he ceased at innocent two,
His blood on a swelling high,
The wicked engorge, blot on,
Their substance brim with lapse.

We expanded your Book,
Lived a ram-rod life ...
Will a comfort counsel hear?
Had to scratch with sweat;
Morsel by morsel,
Spent all our Gospel years
Abetting some rag whisper,
"Yes, Lord,"
Only to be rewarded
By a malaria farewell,
Of my dear Sophie.

Love to meet You then—
Meet You at the answering.

75. TWO PILLARS OF SALT

Manufacture, publish the virus
Of foreign aided sex
Around this globe,
And the nations debate
Who retains, awards,
Copyrights yet another vice.
Admire, sympathize,
Down-rate the X-rating,
And you will set
Yet another pillar of salt.

Ease the digital media,
Whistle them off, run them freely,
Circle your family hearth,
Every eye glued,
And gloom like the silent moon,
Creeps around the adored rooms
Like misty-blue tombs,
Set to meet a second doom.

76. MULTI-COLOURED ONION SKINS

I once saw a maternity ward
On the computer screen
And said, "That isn't clever, glib."
My little daughter was there,
But she stayed on to peep
At the perpetual tube; the
Love-beds that come on easy after ten.
Querulous she got, knotted,
And cut the fruited cake
Before the organ sang beautiful.
Pitied her parts grow and grow,
Till we all saw tears drip drop down
Her chiffon drapes, now not so white.

I taught my boy to pop rubber guns
At innocuous three;
Thought it was a trivial, glib game.
I was asked why I failed to participate
Behind his bars of iron at age sixteen.
Now I'd rather be called square,
And sleep off my kids, calling on our Father
Who dwells in heavenly places,
And make them dream dreams,
Where brides and bridesmaids dress
In multi-coloured onion skins,
And where castles are built of gingerbread.

77. SUPERSEDED LIFE

Gas is for the automobile.
The spirit that we celebrate with;
Quaint crystal glass clicks.
Is it for the liver, as smoke to lungs?
The Almighty would have

Vented each one of us obliging exhausts.

Feed your liver with vitamin Z,
Keep gobbling that blended bacteria's urine,
Keep your heart pumping beyond faithful,
And you will mutate into a jade-coloured ogre.
Twist your clever genes with laser beam,
Clone a chimp, let it speak French, if you can,
Turn your brain to race after the sun.
Without your souls sold out to the Son,
Soon you'll face a breed more conceited
Than Hitler's Germany.

Join God at the drawing board,
Build a super hulk that can make
The Eiffel Tower spin at will;
Make simple nature sing to your crazy song,
But you'll never make apples
Grow in Eden again.

78. BELT OF CAMEL HAIR

What now,
To a fair-class guest,
In a pleasure tour van,
Is marinated locust
In sautéed honey sauce?

79. COLOURED WAVES

Ear to ear, mine is full
Of cathode junk;
The rays that elude after ten.
Been told of many forbidden things,
Even heard the sound of sex.
In a dream, was warned

To keep the dial at position "off;" after ten,
Of synthesized vibes
That even sing to your blood cells.

Eye to eye,
I have seen angles of death,
In coloured waves,
Dance in the vacuum tube.
Have even seen the inside of a woman;
At first was thunder bolt;
To me was thunderbolt.
Now I wonder why we no longer see
Eye to eye with you.

Have read obscene letters; inviting paperbacks,
Now replace the paperbacks of all papers,
Easy talk which replaced our family altar talk.
Been told of many prohibited things,
Been hypnotized to touch
With more than six senses
And wear the hats of demi-gods.
No wonder now,
I can't get any sense of you.

I saw the Ninja guns
Turn Vietnamese flesh into minced meat,
Saw the innocent coconut of a baby
Crack ear to ear; some demon smile,
All in the name of western sausage roll.
They sprayed orange colour fire balls
On entire villages those days.
I saw rice stalks fly those days.

My boy and I watched
Ugly creatures of medieval Europe—were fascinated:

Dinosaurs with human heads, trees that walk and talk,
A feat of modern cinematography and animation.
He watched cups lift off a table on command,
Was told that was elementary magic craft.
Now, the boy wants to do it himself.

My boy and I
Saw high kicks, counter high kicks
On corner B, in the old rail station;
I thought the choreography was great.
He thought the self-defence was warranted,
So he ran to the local YMCA
To join the ranks of black belt heroes,
Who even breathe in Japanese.
Now I have to homage him the eastern bow,
Every time he machos, in my own house.

80. ENOUGH ON YOUR FEET

A car, give it innumerable names, upholster its seats with vicuna wool,
Navigate its wheels GPS touch- button, computerize every mode,
Is still a mobile tin, a Japanese recycled metal.
Alloy its rims; let it talk to you, as you talk to it,
Watch your favourite movie on the back seat; make love, if you must,
Sooner or later it will reel down to the city council's bin.
So long as it does not roll on rails, one day you'll crash it
On a lamppost or a lady licking an ice cream cone.

You dilettante on this, dilettante on that, on feminine-like vanities;
You stopped by a butterfly emblazoned green;
Was fascinated by its weaves, yes weaves.
Clothes and more clothes, droves, wardrobes of them.
Are you Adam's wife, or whoever gave us this din?
Only in a forest do you have an endless supply of leaves.

Shoes, more shoes, a museum of Imelda Marcos' shoes,

Like a horse leach. Can't you have enough on your feet?
Fashion, passion, cassone, the difference is the same.

Houses dreamt in the stars, houses designed on the beach sand,
With Elevations as confused as Gaudi's toys.
Peeped through its Byzantine hallways; was Byzantine,
Lounges that sit you timid and you forget why you came,
Bedrooms that give you more of nightmares,
Than feminine soft-dream and post sauna sleep,
Micro-tech cook places, music like Mo-Town, Cleopatra tubs,
Quilted waterbeds, laced like Victoria Queen.
Chandeliers in Murano glass or Italian quartz,
Hand-beat antique brass inserts in Acacia and ebony wood.
High polished Alabaster that reflect more of your shame,
Italian nudes and Greek gargoyles all in white marble;
You seem not to have enough of those Greek gargoyles.
Niches of eastern dairies—demons, to be precise—
Refurbished once every two years, like mansions for African dictators.

Fly to Bali, sleep on Bali beds; beds that resemble chairs,
Chairs that resemble beds, because who cares, you've paid the price.
Float on tropical surface tension, with Eastern garlands on your neck.
Let the sun soak, sort out any stupidity from your brain, once a year.
You have another trip to Tongaland; it's yours, on a single internet call.

Scandinavian epicurean morsels, Frog-eggs sautéed to taste,
Every herb, Chinese seafood that even walk on your plate,
Lingering English tea served with Sacher Torte and Ricotta Cheesecake,
True, no one desires to eat from bin to bin, no one like eating grass.
When all is said and done, all we need is enough in the fridge,
And a bed that helps you dream and still remember that dream.

Better is a dry morsel and quietness, therewith, than a mansion full of strife.
God is not intimidated by mansions filled with precious knick knacks;

In fact, He hopes our houses are full, not with ignoble clay and
    cheap plasticware,
But furnished as if we were indeed children of the Most High God.
So when it comes to Murano glass and Italian quartz, I'd say Amen.
He desires that our Alabaster cups be filled to the overflowing,
Overflowing to some poor saucer somewhere, to lend and not to borrow.
Alloyed rims or not, He has taught us to die only for the things that keep
    their gleam,
Which moths, credit crunches, don't eat, or fall as the charts fall.
And to bank with The New Jerusalem Bank Incorporated.

81. UNFAMILIAR FINGER

Who is that dream girl who invades my wedded bed
Night after night, picking me flowers on lovers' lane again,
Tempting me back to my bachelorhood trauma?
The time when I was looking for a finger to ring.
Must be a demon dressed like a college girl,
Mocking my wedded bed and altar vows.
I can't see your face clearly, though you smile,
Challenge me to smile back to your college smile.
I am glad I rebuke you for mocking my altar vows;
Woke up, refused to slide a ring down an unfamiliar finger.

ABOUT THE AUTHOR

Silver O'City was born on August 26th, 1950, in Northern Uganda. He grew up in Mican (Mission) – Gulu. Silver began his poetry writing for school magazines while he was attending Kabalega Senior Secondary School, in Masindi. He later attended Busoga College Mwiri, Jinja. In 1972, he went on to study Architecture at the Nairobi University, Kenya, where he obtained a first class honours degree.

In Nairobi Silver pioneered Contemporary Gospel Music in the region through his band, The Trekkers, leading the group for six years. He also wrote and directed a popular youth musical call Evidence. In 1979, Mr. O'city went to Scotland to study Urban and Regional Planning, at the University of Edinburgh where he obtained a Masters of Philosophy degree.

Mr. O'City is a multi-talented person. In addition to running his architectural office in Kampala, he and his wife Harriet O'City are involved in farming, export of crafts and interior accessories. They are also heavily involved in their church ministry and leadership. They have three equally talent adult children.